Please renew/return this item by the last date shown.

So that your telephone call is charged at local rate, please call the numbers as set out below:

	From Area codes 01923 or 0208:	From the rest of Herts:
Renewals:	01923 471373	01438 737373
Enquiries:	01923 471333	01438 737333
Minicom:	01923 471599	01438 737599

L32b

TOBACCO CULTURE
A D.I.Y. GUIDE

This book is dedicated to Hubert Appleyard
in appreciation of much advice
and encouragement in the early days.

Tobacco Culture
A D.I.Y. Guide

by

GUY N. SMITH

THE SPUR PUBLICATIONS COMPANY
Hill Brow, LISS, Hampshire GU33 7PU

Photoset by Petaprint, Petersfield
Printed and bound by
Redwood Burn Limited
Trowbridge & Esher

Published by
THE SPUR PUBLICATIONS COMPANY
HILL BROW, LISS, HAMPSHIRE

Contents

List of Illustrations

Acknowledgement

My thanks to Fred Ellett who provided the basic sketches from which all the drawings and diagrams in this book were made.

Guy N. Smith

PUBLISHERS NOTE

As emphasized by the Author, *Tobacco Culture* in its widest sense, is a personal affair between the smoker and the tobacco he grows. Accordingly, the views expressed are those of the Author. The fact that tobacco smoking can constitute a health hazard should not be overlooked.

CHAPTER 1

A Useful Hobby

INTRODUCTION

Few people appreciate the tobacco-growing potential of the British Isles. *Nicotiana,* the flowering variety, decorates many gardens, yet the various other species will grow equally as well. Whatever you smoke, pipe, cigarette, or cigar; whatever your taste, strong, medium or mild, there is a variety to suit *you* . . . and you can grow it!

In 1948 tobacco-growing for *personal* consumption was sanctioned by Parliament. The only proviso was a limit of 25 lbs of cured leaf per person. That in itself was extremely generous. On average each plant yields two ounces of cured leaf. So, to grow 1 lb of smokeable tobacco one will require 8 plants, say ten, to allow for waste during harvesting and curing. Your legal limit then is 250 plants, spaced 2 ft. apart, and 3 ft. between the rows. In order to grow the maximum amount you would need a garden or allotment 150 ft. long by 10 ft. wide. The work involved would make it a full-time job.

More realistically, it is better to estimate your smoking requirements, and grow enough plants to meet this annually. Four ounces per week would require a minimum of one hundred plants, and that is enough for any man to tend.

In order not to infringe any Customs and Excise regulations you must not sell or even give away cured leaf. Even offering a friend a fill from your pouch technically puts you on the wrong side of the law. Seed or plants, though, may be sold.

The price of commercial tobacco is increasing annually. Standard blends at the time of writing retail at about 70p per ounce. In 1960 the same brand could be purchased for five shillings. It has almost trebled! Surely, that in itself is enough for any lover of the weed to take action. There are three alternatives open:

1. to cut down on tobacco consumption to meet individual pockets;

2. to stop smoking altogether;

3. **to grow your own tobacco.**

Experiments are being conducted on a commercial level to determine the success in growing tobacco in Britain. The results will probably not be made public for a long time yet. However, it is sufficient to say that the idea has not been ignored by the big combines. That, in itself, is heartening to any would-be home-grower.

CLIMATIC INFLUENCES

The climate of this country is changing. We have had two scorching summers in succession, and one weather-expert suggests that this may be the pattern for the next fifty years. That may not be good news to farmers and market-gardeners, but it is certainly heartening to the tobacco-grower. Up until this change came about the big drawback to tobacco-growing was the absence of prolonged sunshine. Plants which cannot be put out into the open until the danger of frosts are over have to be matured and ready for harvesting by the end of August at the very latest. Consequently, in the past years we had leaves hanging up to dry which were not yet ready for harvesting. A wet September meant that they had no chance to dry, and many enthusiasts were discouraged by a crop of mildewed leaf which ended up on the compost-heap. Very few persevered. I was one of those who did, and that is the reason I have written this book.

MAKING A START

I grew my first tobacco in 1960, and smoked it out of sheer obstinacy. My only guidance were the instructions on the packet of seed. I had no equipment, whatsoever. In effect, the leaf was just grown and dried. I had no knowledge of curing, so the finished product was cut up with a pair of scissors, moistened with a slice of potato in the pouch, and smoked with determination. Possibly oak leaves would have served just as well. I pretended I enjoyed it. Those around me made it quite clear that *they* did not!

However, I tried again the following year, this time under the guidance of Hubert Appleyard, then librarian to the City of Lichfield. His methods, although somewhat unorthodox when compared with the many instructional leaflets which were to follow over the next decade, produced what I consider to be the nearest possible to a commercial brand. His experience and my experiments have brought their reward.

ESTABLISHING A STANDARD

Whilst we must not always use the proprietary brands as our yardstick, their popularity has been proved over the years, and we must try to strike a happy medium, something which is pleasant to the palate, but with a greater degree of *pure* leaf. One has only to sample imported brands to become aware of the adulteration which takes place in the search for new flavours. *Flavouring can often disguise poor leaf.* With our own tobacco at least we are aware of the quality which we smoke, and, more important, **the nicotine content is lower.** In the description of my own method of curing, later in this book, you will see how the harmful nicotine is extracted from the tobacco. In fact, a local gardener relies upon me for annual supplies of this 'waste' for use as an insecticide.

So, the advantages of growing your own tobacco are manifold. Economy, purity. and last but not least, *satisfaction.* Every time that you light your pipe, cigarette, or cigar, you will experience the same satisfaction as the gardener who sits down at the table to an entirely home-produced meal. You will have created your favourite brand of tobacco. It will be unique. Nowhere in the world will there be another *exactly* like it. You will have achieved individualism in a world that is succumbing daily to new monopolies.

CHAPTER 2

Cultivation I

PREPARATION OF SOIL

Almost any soil will grow tobacco, regardless of the advice given in many leaflets. Some advocate heavy soil, others light and well-drained. The test is whether or not your garden will produce a crop of vegetables. **If so, then it will grow tobacco.**

As with any soil, you must prepare and feed it well in advance. Ground that is dug and matured in the autumn is always preferable. I build up my compost throughout the summer months and then once autumn is here, and the ground is cleared, I dig all of this in. Good deep digging is essential, although there is no need to break up the clods of earth as the more frost that penetrates and kills pests the better. Pests will be dealt with later under a separate heading. Of course, farm manure is even better if you are in a position to obtain it. Sometimes I use both compost and manure. The more you dig in, the better chance you will have of a bumper crop of tobacco.

Leave your tobacco patch to weather until the spring. Then, in March or April fork it over lightly, and break up those clods. I was fortunate some years ago in obtaining an obsolete garden hand-plough. Providing that the ground has been dug in the autumn it is easy to use, and I generally turn my plot over in about ten minutes. Of course, a cultivator is fine if you have one.

I am not keen on the use of lime on the ground where tobacco is going to be planted. All too often, particularly in a dry winter, it is not absorbed into the soil, and is inclined to burn the lower leaves of plants which come into contact with it. If you decide that the use of lime is necessary then it is a good idea to water it well in.

Take some care in the planning of your tobacco plot. Remember that your plants will need to be two feet apart with three feet in between each row. Any attempt at cramming will result in smaller plants, and consequently smaller leaves. Get it all worked out beforehand. Draw up a plan.

COMPOST

Some thought must be given to the building of your compost heap. All too often growers are inclined to regard this as more of a rubbish-tip on to which every unwanted item of household or garden waste goes. Little do they realise that in many cases they are doing more harm than good. Half the contents will not rot down, and, consequently, when it is time to dig the compost into the ground they are filling their trench with something which will hinder the growth of the plants. Let us first consider waste which is *unsuitable* for compost before looking at that which will benefit the ground:—

1. **Rhubarb leaves.** Under no circumstances should

these be included. Their only benefit as a compost is amongst the stools from which they have been pulled.

2. **Stalks from cabbage or other greenstuffs.** These are slow to rot down even after having lain throughout the winter. By the time they are capable of being beneficial to the soil you will be harvesting your tobacco leaves! A common mistake by many gardeners is to dig in the stalks of the greens which they pull up in the early spring, leaving the roots attached. As a result the tobacco plot is likely to have cabbages, sprouts or broccoli growing in it by about mid-June!

3. **Hedge-cuttings.** The branches will not rot down for a long time, and they are likely to impede the root growth of your tobacco. Some hedge leaves, such as privet, are nutritious to soil whilst laurel is not. In the case of a mixed hedge one could be cancelling out the other so the best method is to burn all your hedge-cuttings and then put the ash on your compost heap.

4. **Lawn cuttings treated with weedkiller.** Although lawn cuttings form the basis of many compost heaps, if you have used *any* lawn weedkiller then it is advisable to deposit the contents of your grass-box in some place where it is not likely to do any harm for at least the three cuts following the dressing.

These are the main items to *avoid* in any compost heap, whether intended for tobacco growing or general gardening.

Now let us study those which will be beneficial:

(a) **Untreated lawn cuttings.** Depending upon the size of your lawn these will provide a regular compost. They rot down to an excellent mulch, but must be kept moist at all times. During a spell of severe drought they will become mouldy if neglected, and the last thing the tobacco-grower wants to encourage is mould.

(b) **Potato and fruit parings.** These are ideal as they hold moisture and rot quickly.

(c) **Vegetables which have gone to seed.** Every garden experiences this, particularly in dry weather. Beet, lettuce, swedes, turnips etc., can be pulled and provide useful compost, but inspect them first, and always remove the roots. You do not want to breed garden pests in your compost heap.

(d) **Tobacco leaves and side-shoots from the previous season.** These rot down well and the small nicotine content in them discourages pests.

The items mentioned above should provide you with an excellent compost heap. There are, of course, many others which you can include, but if you are in any doubt as to their suitability then consult a good gardening-book. Generally the harmful matter will be listed.

We are now aware of what and what not to include in the compost heap, but merely to throw them into an untidy pile in a forgotten corner of the garden is not sufficient. A compost heap is something which has to be constructed and tended carefully if it is to give the best results.

Construction and Care of a Compost Heap.

A compost heap needs to be sited somewhere where it is exposed to the elements. An overhanging tree or bush will keep the moisture off it, and during the winter months the frost will help to kill those pests which have decided to use it for hibernation. Therefore, where possible choose an open space, preferably away from dwelling places so that any obnoxious odours do not cause offence to others. A compost heap should not give off unpleasant smells, as in the case of a heap of farm manure, but rotting substances can hardly be considered aromatic at close quarters.

First, dig a foundation which need be no more than six inches deep. You must determine the size of your compost heap in relation to the waste which you expect to have, and the area which it must serve. It is a good idea to enclose it with wire-netting held firmly in place by stakes. I have seen sheets of corrugated iron used for this, but this is inclined to stifle the compost, preventing ventilation, hindering the process of rotting, and causing mould. A neat compost heap is unlikely to be an eyesore in an attractive garden.

Once your structure is completed you can commence filling the foundation, *evenly,* then forking it and watering it lightly. Lawn cuttings are ideal. As in the building of a house, the foundation is important to the rest of the structure. The items advised against could not only disturb the structure, but affect the organic reaction throughout.

When the humus is a foot or so deep, a light covering of *good* soil will be beneficial. Build the compost heap in

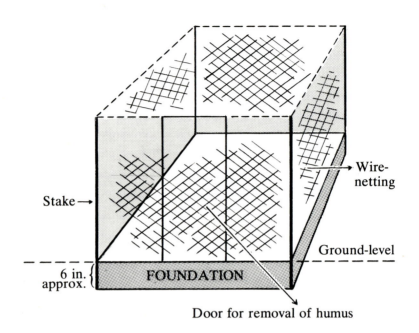

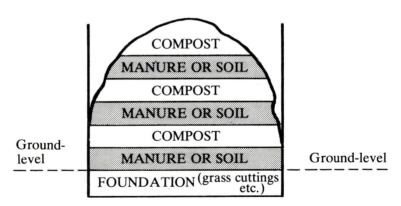

Diagram 2.1 Suggested layout of compost heap,
alternate layers of manure and compost.

layers on these lines, watering it frequently.

I have deliberately avoided a mention of dead leaves in either my "do's" or "don'ts" of the compost heap. Whilst leaf-mould is generally excellent for the garden there is always the risk of inducing pests into the soil, particularly after a long dry summer when many trees have been blighted with a variety of pests. I prefer to burn my leaves, and then use the ash on the compost heap.

It will be twelve months before your compost is ready for digging into the soil. Some gardeners use *two* heaps. In many cases this is not possible owing to lack of space so in order to make the best use of the humus at your disposal it is advisable to use that which is at the bottom of the pile first. Using a fork remove as much as necessary only, as carefully as you can. Some kind of a small 'door' can be constructed initially in your wire-netting enclosure for this purpose, but, there again, this will depend on the size of your compost heap.

It is often a good idea to leave your compost heap lightly covered with unslaked lime during the winter months. Peat moss or bracken will also serve. If it is apparent that your compost is not rotting down, something which is inclined to happen in periods of drought no matter how frequently you water, then salt, soda, and lime added at intervals, and watered, will assist this.

MANURE

The manuring of ground is something also which must not be undertaken haphazardly. Tobacco grows well in either cow or horse dung, but you will have to make your choice according to which suits your ground better. It will be necessary to experiment, but a few hints on the general application may be helpful.

There are two ways of digging manure into your ground. You can either fill the trenches as you dig the ground, or else spread the dung liberally first, and then dig it in. I prefer the former because you obtain a concentration of manure, possibly six inches deep below the surface soil, whilst with the latter you obtain only a shallow depth.

On light soil it is preferable to use partially decayed manure and dig it in during the very early spring. On heavier soils fresher manure is better providing it is dug in during the autumn. **On no account plant your tobacco straight into fresh manure.**

Soil which has been manured in this way about November will retain its moisture right up until the time of planting. It is also a good idea, if you have a plot of ground clear by the end of August, to sow it with mustard seed. As soon as the mustard begins to flower, dig it in, and this will help to retain humus in the soil.

One other point worth mentioning is that if your family keeps tame rabbits, the straw and dung from the hutch is ideal for your compost heap. In many ways I consider it to be equally as good as horse or cow except that the quantity is insufficient to manure the whole patch.

Manure and compost are a complement to each other. If you have a readily available supply of manure then it is an excellent idea to include it in your compost heap in alternate layers. You will obtain excellent humus in this way.

FERTILIZERS

When considering the use of fertilizers for your tobacco plot there are three main factors to bear in mind:—

1. Potash promotes growth.
2. Nitrogen aids yield.
3. Phosphate strengthens roots and will improve the quality of the leaves.

None of these must be considered as a substitute for either compost or manure. There are fertilizers which combine all three, and these are generally scattered around the base of the growing plant, taking care not to bring it into direct contact with the stem. Phosphate alone is best scattered over the tobacco plot a fortnight before planting out, and then raked in.

Bone meal or dried blood can be scattered in the bottom of the trenches during digging, deep enough so that they do not come into contact with the tender roots of the plants until the tobacco grows down into them.

You may have to experiment for several seasons with fertilizers before discovering the one which suits your soil and tobacco plants best. Below is a list of *mineral* fertilizers, the soil to which they are suited, and the correct time of application:—

Basic Slag. A top dressing for heavy soil. *Autumn/winter.*

Kainit (potash), Light soil. To be forked in during the *Autumn.*

Nitrate of Potash. A top dressing for all types of soil. *Spring.*

Nitrate of Soda. A top dressing for all types of soil. *Spring.*

Nitro Chalk. To be forked in heavy soil during *spring and summer.*

Sulphate of Ammonia. A top dressing for *spring and summer.*

Sulphate of Potash. A top dressing for heavy soil. *Spring and autumn.*

Superphosphate of Lime. Unsuitable for acid soil. Most other soils. *Spring and autumn.*

Once you are producing good results it is inadvisable to experiment further and risk a bad season. Above all, bear in mind *crop rotation.* Use a different plot for your tobacco each year otherwise you will drain your ground of all its goodness.

CHAPTER 3

Cultivation II

VARIETIES

There are only four main varieties of tobacco worth considering which suit both the British climate and the needs of the average smoker.

Hungarian

Tall plants with large thin leaves. It is suitable for making either very strong cigarettes or for use as cigar wrappers.

Burley

A very hardy plant that is also wind-resistant and suitable for growing in areas which are unsheltered. The leaves are slim in texture, producing a mild smoke suitable for cigarette-making. Surely this is the cigarette smoker's choice.

Havana

This is a particularly dark leaf, and, as the name suggests, is the ideal choice for the one who makes his own cigars. An outer wrapping of Hungarian leaf with a Havana filling is possibly the best blend there is for home-made cigars.

Brazilian

The ideal pipe-tobacco. Very large leaves, and also

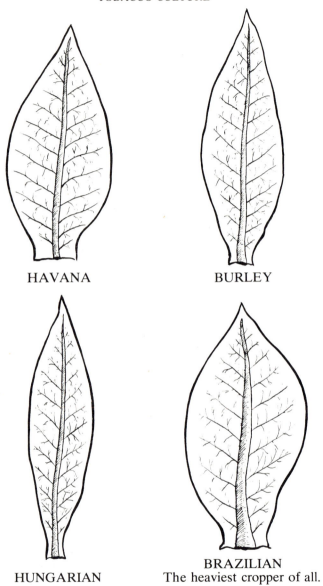

HAVANA

BURLEY

HUNGARIAN

BRAZILIAN
The heaviest cropper of all.

Diagram 3.1 Varieties of Leaf.

16

wind-resistant. I have grown this variety for the past five years, and find its heavy yield advantageous where space is limited. It is also suitable as a cigar 'filler'. One of the main features of Brazilian is that it has plenty of 'body' to it, and produces a cool, slow-burning smoke with a unique flavour.

Therefore, my choice would be as follows:—

Hungarian for cigarettes, **Havana** for cigars, and **Brazilian** for the pipe.

However, smoking is so very personal that one hardly dares to generalise. A man who prefers a very mild pipe-tobacco may well decide upon Hungarian, whilst the one who has been accustomed to American cigarettes or cigarillos would choose to roll either Havana or Brazilian in his papers.

It may be advisable to experiment with all four varieties at your first attempt, but once they are hanging up to dry be sure to mark your various lines because once the leaves are dried, the difference between them will not be apparent to the novice. You may well find that you develop a preference for a certain blend, and then, to your annoyance, find that you do not know which variety it is! Thus, experiment with varieties in your first year, and then make your choice.

SEED OR PLANTS?

The tobacco-grower finds himself faced with the same problem as that of the amateur poultry-rearer who cannot make up his mind whether to hatch eggs or to buy in day-old chicks. Is it preferable to grow from seed or buy plants from one of the nurseries which specialise in tobacco?

I would advocate growing from your own seed in almost every instance. Firstly, plants are expensive, averaging about 80p per dozen. Your aim for economy is already receiving its first set-back! Secondly, unless you are able to collect your plants personally from the nursery then they will have to endure two or three days in the post. Even when well-packed in moist peat this does check the excellent start which they have had, and on the one occasion when I purchased plants in this way I found that their growth was so retarded that they barely caught up in time for the harvest.

Seed is cheap from a variety of sources. Many of the country's leading seedsmen advertise them in their catalogues at about 15p per packet. One packet is ample for the seeds are so minute that you will have more than enough for your requirements. Better still, after your first year take your own seed from your plants. This is best done immediately the plants have died off, before the autumn dampness sets in.

TAKING YOUR OWN SEED

I usually take my seed in mid-October. It is only necessary to leave one plant in the ground. One pod in itself will provide you with as much as you will get in the average purchased packet.

Do not break the pod open to take the seed. Pick the pods as you would do peas, and hang them up in a dry but well-ventilated place until February. I use a paper carrier-bag for this purpose, and inspect them at weekly intervals just to make sure that no mishap has befallen them. By the time you are ready to sow your crop, the seeds will have fallen out into the bottom of the bag, and you will probably find that you have a couple of saucers full.

The advantage of taking your own seed is that it is already acclimatised to the local soil, and the quality of your leaf will be greatly improved by this.

SOWING

Sow your seed in gentle heat towards the end of February or at the beginning of March. No sooner and no later. I remember the first time that I took my own seed and set them in January in my enthusiasm. I was thrilled with their rapid progress until it suddenly became obvious to me that they were too far advanced. It was too early to put them out in the open, and as a result they outgrew themselves, weakened, and wilted.

A late sowing means that your plants will not be ready to put outside at the end of May. Remember, they only have a limited time in which to mature.

Care must be taken with sowing. It is fine if you have a heated greenhouse, but otherwise you will obtain excellent results by sowing in boxes or pots indoors. A constant temperature of 60° F is essential throughout, and I find that placed in the vicinity of one of my central-heating radiators the seeds germinate and grow as well as in any greenhouse.

It is essential not to sow too thickly. This is easily done with such minute seeds, and the only way to obtain even distribution is to mix with an equal amount of sand. Dense sowing will result in weakened seedlings before they are ready to prick out.

Sterilised soil is best to give your seedlings a good healthy start. Sow the seed on the surface, and keep it moist. It is a good idea where possible to stand your pots or seedbox in a tray of water. Watering from the bottom is always more efficient than sprinkling.

Some growers cover their pots or boxes with a sheet of brown paper, or else keep them in a darkened place. I have found from experience that this is totally unnecessary, and also one is inclined to forget to water them if they are not continually in sight. Mine always germinate on the window-sill in the living-room.

GERMINATION

Seed usually germinates within about a week. After that it will grow fast, and if you have been over-enthusiastic, and sown a little too early, then it is a good idea to move them away to an even gentler heat. This happened to me only a couple of years ago, and by transferring the pots to the opposite side of the room, away from the radiator, I slowed their growth so that they were ready for pricking out at just about the right time.

It is always a good idea when growing from your own seed to test for germination a few weeks before you are ready to commence sowing your main crop. In this way you will determine whether or not your seed is sufficiently fertile. Otherwise you may find yourself in the frustrating position of trying to buy seed at the last moment, and a delay could make all the difference between a good and a poor crop.

PRICKING OUT

There are no hard and fast rules regarding pricking out. Basically, I carry this out when the seedlings are an inch or so high, and have the appearance of becoming choked. However, pricking-out is **essential** for good healthy plants. At the time of writing I had a surplus box of seedlings (my 'spares') which I did not bother to prick out. Rather than waste them I put them in odd spaces in the herbacious border, but it was apparent within the first fortnight that their growth was much inferior to my main crop in the vegetable garden.

One point to note here, and I make no apology over the fact that I shall repeat this in another section of the book, **do not handle seedlings immediately after having filled your pipe from your pouch of commercial tobacco.** I cannot give any reason for this other than that I suspect that the tar from the latter burns the former, and they are inclined to 'yellow' where they have been touched. It will also give them a sickly appearance for a week or two, and the loss of progress may mean that their maturity will be retarded.

Prick them out in the same way that you would do lettuces or any other seedlings. Thirty to a box is ample. I always use John Innes seed compost, and for the remaining month of their 'indoor confinement' you will see them grow rapidly.

Another point worth mentioning here is that if you are growing tobacco in any quantity in a greenhouse then it is inadvisable to have other plants in the same enclosure. I heard of one man who lost all his bedding-out plants for this reason, and I can only attribute it to the nicotine in the air.

PLANTING OUT

I always plant out as near to May 31st as possible. By this time there should be little risk of frost, and the plants will need every day possible to mature before it is harvest time. I prefer the word 'mature' to 'ripen' as I shall explain in a later stage of this book.

Tobacco plants have a reputation for being very vulnerable to frost. However, in my fifteen years of tobacco growing I can never once recall having lost a single plant because of this. In fact, I consider them to be quite hardy as the following account will show:

On May 30th, 1975, I planted out sixty tobacco plants. It was warm and raining steadily, ideal conditions. By June 1st the weather had changed drastically. It became bitterly cold, and one could not go outside without a topcoat. Then, on June 2nd, here in the Midlands, *it snowed!* I stood in the living-room window and watched the garden rapidly becoming white over. Some two inches fell altogether, drifting on to my tobacco plants until they were completely buried.

I resigned myself to a total loss, and contemplated my tobacco bill over the coming year. In fact, I almost decided to give up smoking!

The following day we underwent another drastic change in climatic conditions. The sun shone, the snow melted, and within a week we had embarked upon a heatwave! As for my plants, they showed not the slightest sign of their ordeal. Admittedly, there had been no frost, but I doubt whether tobacco-growers in Britain had ever experienced such conditions before.

Nevertheless, beware of frost, and regard May 31st as 'planting-out day'.

Handle your plants with care, wash your hands if you have just been in contact with commercial tobacco, and do not try to rush the job. Nothing any good was ever done in a hurry!

My first move is to dig the required number of holes with a spade, drop some manure in each, and then lightly cover over with soil so that the tender roots are not immediately brought into contact with a powerful fertilizer or manure.

I then place each plant into a hole, cover the roots, and press the earth down firmly around it. It depends upon the moisture content of the soil whether or not I 'puddle' them in. If it is necessary to do this then I make sure that I do not use water which has been freshly drawn from the tap. A rain-water butt is an ideal source, but failing this it is best to draw the water the day before, and let it stand until you are ready to use it, preferably in the direct rays of the sun if at all possible.

Make sure that soil is not clinging to the leaves of the plants. Dirty leaves do not grow as well as clean ones. and are inclined to become weighed down and embedded in the ground. It is your lower leaves which will produce your heaviest crop, so look after them.

Your crop is now planted, but if you think that you can just forget about it until August then you will not reap

Figure 1 Brazilian tobacco plants,
about a month after planting out.

much of a harvest. There is an awful lot of work to be done in the meantime.

For the first couple of weeks your plants will show little or no progress. This is quite usual, and there is no cause for alarm. All that has happened is that the process of planting-out has checked them, but once they have rooted properly they will show a rapid growth.

FEEDING PLANTS

In the meantime your plants need feeding regularly. The manure beneath them is not sufficient on its own. In this respect they are similar to tomatoes.

Saltpetre is an ideal dressing during the growing period, applying a teaspoonful to each plant every fortnight or three weeks. A garden fertilizer containing Nitrogen, Phosphoric Acid, and Potash, applied weekly, will give them an added boost.

Once they start to grow rapidly the soil should be heaped up at the base of the roots in the same way that one would do in the case of potatoes. It is also essential to remove all flower-buds and secondary shoots so that maximum concentration is given to the leaves. Large leaves are your aim. Far better is it to have ten long, broad leaves than twenty small ones. Not only will they mature quicker, but they will be a lot easier to harvest. There is nothing more time-consuming and demoralising than having line after line of small leaves hanging up to dry.

Obviously, you will have sited your plants in a place where they receive the maximum amount of sunlight. However, it is not always possible to combine shelter with this, and you may find yourself troubled with strong winds. If your plants are snapped off then there is nothing you can do to rectify the situation. Prevention is always better than cure, so if your plants are in a particularly exposed area then stake them, and take no chances. Brazilian and Burley will stand up to most winds, but it is better to be on the safe side.

If the weather is exceptionally dry then water your plants daily even when they have attained a height of three or four feet. Every bit of extra growth that you can force out of them means more tobacco for your pipe, but ensure that you do not cake your roots with dried mud. **Water frequently.**

PESTS

Like every other plant which grows in your garden, tobacco is vulnerable to pests, particularly slugs. Slugs seem attracted to nicotine, and their depredations can be noted in the first week or so after planting. One morning you will go out into the garden to discover that one of your small plants has been eaten almost down to the stem. Unless you take action at once, by the following morning you will have lost two plants.

Slug pellets from garden suppliers are generally effective, but I have found that sometimes slugs prefer nicotine to whatever lure is contained in the poison! Also, in dry weather these pellets are less consistent. The best protection for your tobacco plants is soot at the base of the stems, but, here again, care must be exercised. **Old soot must be used if you are not to scorch your tobacco.**

During a recent heatwave in the Midlands we experienced a plague of greenfly. Now greenfly are not harmful to tobacco in the same way that they are to other crops. They will not eat the plant because of the nicotine content, so do not panic if you discover your tobacco covered with this blight. It would appear that they only use it as a temporary 'resting place'.

The best friends that the tobacco-grower has are frogs and toads, particularly the latter. If you can persuade Mister Toad to stay in the vicinity of your patch you will not have much trouble with slugs. They will just disappear. He is far more effective than any amount of pellets or soot.

TREATMENT OF GROWING LEAVES

The more your plants grow, the more attention the leaves will need. Often some of the extreme lower ones will become yellowed and wilt. They will fall to the ground, and become covered with soil. It is important that they are removed for the benefit of the others. This condition is caused by lack of sunlight as the upper foliage screens it from them.

You will notice also that the upper leaves collect a host of various seeds that float through the air, particularly dandelion balls. These are not harmful in themselves, but they will cling to the leaves right through the process of curing, and I have even found them in the final processed tobacco!

There is only one way to combat this, and that is by carefully sponging each leaf with luke-warm soapy water. It is a time-consuming task, but it will be well

Figure 2 Sponging leaves.
Photo: Lance Smith

worth it in the end. Be careful how you handle the leaves, though, for every broken rib means a leaf ruined. Place the open hand beneath each leaf, sponging gently towards you, and then reverse your hold so that you can do the same to the underneath.

The sticky texture of the leaves will catch small insects, too, particularly in the latter stages of growth when the plants have almost attained maturity. 'Resting' greenfly will become trapped, and the only way in which they will be removed is by sponging.

Sometimes strong winds will almost turn the leaves over so that their undersides are visible. No actual harm is done by this so long as the ribs have not been broken or severed from the stem, but it is the work of only a few minutes to replace them. It is always preferable that they hang naturally from the plant.

Side-shoots will be noticed from July onwards. These are in the form of additional branches with small leaves that will never reach maturity. They are merely absorbing growth that should be concentrated into the large leaves, and should be removed at once.

WEEDING

It will be noticed that once tobacco plants assume a growth of any size, few weeds grow beneath them. However, as in any form of gardening, the fewer weeds that you have, the better. These will only trouble you in the early stages, and all weeding should be done by hand. Hoeing will disturb the roots of the tobacco.

Figure 3 Surplus plants can be grown in flower borders.

ADJOINING CROPS

It is as well not to overlook the planning of the remainder of your garden or allotment when fixing the site for your tobacco 'plantation'. For instance, a row of runner beans, once they assume full growth, could well shield your tobacco from the sunlight. Likewise, your tobacco leaves will spread and overhang other vegetables. I once lost a row of early cauliflowers when they became covered by the lower leaves of my tobacco.

If possible, allow a margin of four feet on either side of your tobacco plants where nothing is planted. It may seem a waste in the early stages before the growth has got under way, but once those immense (hopefully!) leaves are growing from the plants you will appreciate the wisdom of space.

LEFT-OVER PLANTS

Most tobacco growers find when they have finished planting that they have a few plants left over. Unless one has an *enthusiastic* friend who would appreciate them as a gift, it is always worthwhile trying to fit them in somewhere in the garden. They may not grow as well as the main crop, but an extra pound of leaf is always welcome. I have even grown them on the front rockery, and aroused the suspicion of passers-by that I am cultivating cannabis!

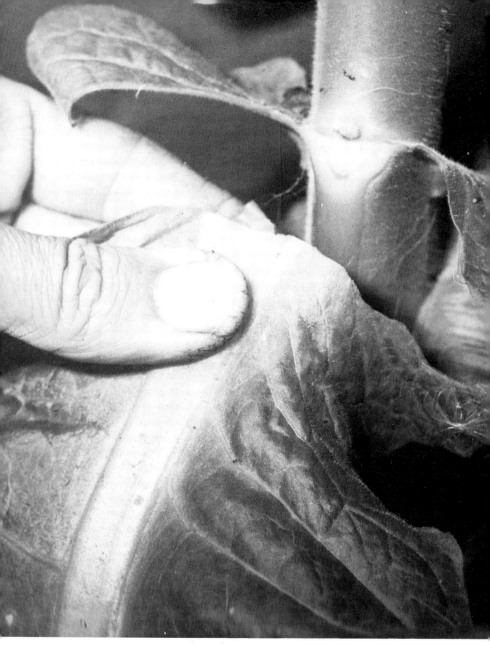

Figure 4 Harvesting Leaves
Method of removing leaf from plant. *Photo: Lance Smith*

CHAPTER 4

Harvesting

WHEN TO PICK THE LEAVES

Every tobacco-grower is relieved when at last August arrives, and it is time to harvest the crop that he has nurtured since the previous March. In some ways, though, I experience a feeling of sadness. Not only is it a sign that summer is waning, but also that my tobacco culture will be confined to indoors from now onwards.

I always reckon to take my initial batch of leaves by the end of the first week in August. Harvesting is a gradual process. Depending on climatic conditions it may be completed in a fortnight, or it may take a month. However, no leaf picked after the beginning of September will make good smoking tobacco. The nights are becoming damper, early morning mists are in evidence, and the chances of leaf drying successfully are remote. Therefore pick *all* your leaf before the end of August.

'When are the leaves ripe?' is a question which I am constantly asked.

I have mentioned earlier in this book that I do not recognise the term 'ripe'. Some growers maintain that leaf is not ready for picking until it becomes mottled. If I

Figure 5 Leaves ready for Harvesting.
Photo: Lance Smith

adhered to that rule at least 25% of my crop would be harvested in September, and never have a chance to dry properly.

The moment August arrives I prepare to harvest. The first step is to remove *all* leaves with a length in excess of eighteen inches. Normally leaves will average eighteen inches to two feet long, their breadth being determined by the variety. For instance, Brazilian have a width of approximately ten to twelve inches. Hungarian are much more slender, say, eight or nine.

There is only one correct way to pick tobacco leaves. I have even seen some amateur growers cutting them off with a knife! Hold the stem of the leaf where it joins the plant, and pull sharply downwards. The leaf will come away easily in your hand. Be sure to hold the leaves flat as you move amongst your plants, and keep them all facing the same way as it will make it so much easier for you when you come to hang them up to dry.

The whole operation does not take very long. Indeed, my first gathering from sixty plants last season took me about a quarter of an hour. Bear in mind that these will be your best leaves. They are fully mature, and they will have ample time to dry before the early autumnal mists set in. You will note also that the majority of the leaves do show some signs of mottling, and are 'ripe' by conventional standards. At this stage, too, the nicotine content is high, as will be evident from your black sticky hands. They will require a thorough washing and scrubbing before they are clean again.

Do not be tempted to pick the smaller leaves, those that *almost* match up to the dimensions which you have

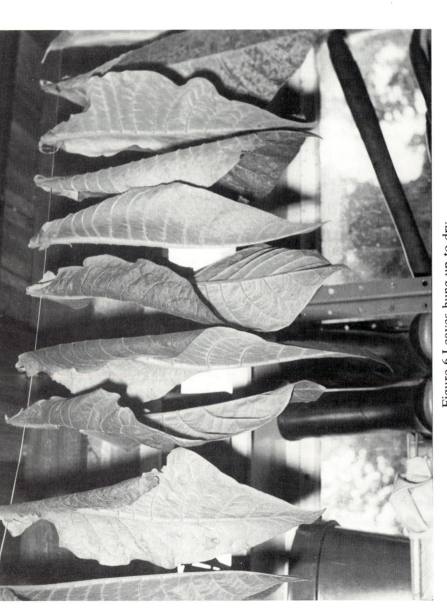

Figure 6 Leaves hung up to dry.
Note spacing, and leaves 'front to back'. *Photo: Lance Smith*

in mind. They will be ready in another week, and by picking them now you will only deprive yourself of a few ounces of smoking tobacco.

Never harvest in wet weather. Your leaves must be perfectly dry before picking, otherwise you are inviting mildew at a very early stage.

Some growers pull up the whole plant about mid-August, leave them in an outhouse to dry off, and then take the total crop about a week later. Although I have proof of a fairly satisfactory end product, it is not a method which appeals to me. I consider it wasteful. Half the leaves should have been gathered a fortnight previously whilst the other half have been deprived of a couple of weeks' growth.

So, your first lot of leaves are gathered. Handle them with great care for damage is easily done. Midribs can break, or leaves tear at the slightest mis-handling. Lay them flat on a table, and then sponge them individually with warm soapy water just as you did at intervals whilst they were growing. Not only will you remove the last of the dandelion balls etc., but you will also improve their look, and give them a nice sheen. There is little to be gained by this appearance, except that it helps to boost the confidence of every tobacco-grower. Nothing looks worse than rows of dirty leaves hanging up in a garage or outhouse. They do not inspire one to be meticulous with the following batches.

HANGING UP TO DRY

The place chosen as your 'drying room' needs to have a current of air passing through it constantly. It is no

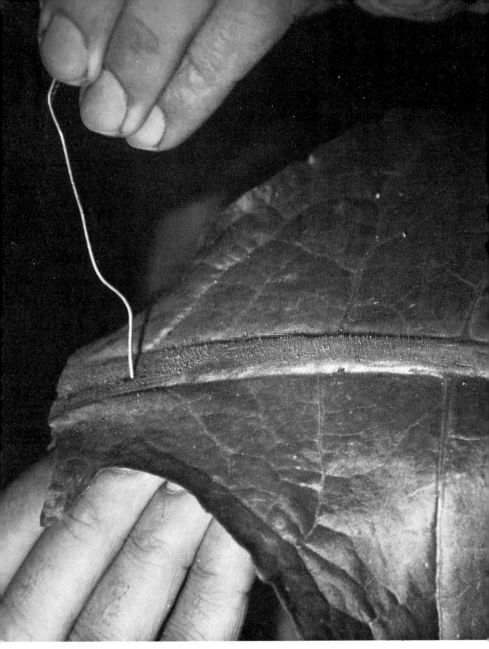

Figure 7 Pushing wire through stem of leaf.
Photo: Lance Smith

good stringing leaf up in a shed, shutting the door, and hoping for the best. I lost my whole crop in my early years in this way. It had certainly been a bumper harvest, and the leaf was drying nicely in the garage towards the end of September. On the first of October I was going on a holiday for a week so I locked the doors, and looked forward to some choice leaf on my return. On my home-coming I was destined for a very nasty shock. The garage smelled damp and musty, and every leaf was covered with mildew! Months of painstaking work had been wasted.

It is a common fallacy that a greenhouse, conservatory, or any place that has a glass roof which admits constant sunshine is ideal for drying. Admittedly the tobacco dries more quickly, but it becomes so brittle that it crumbles to the slightest touch. One is likely to end up with boxes of broken tobacco that is little use for anything except cigar-filler . . . and there will be no leaves suitable for use as outer wrappers!

It is not necessary to produce that rich golden colour which is always portrayed in commercial tobacco advert-isements. **The colour does not matter so long as the leaf is properly dried.** Indeed, probably 20% of the leaf which I cure (usually from my final harvesting) still has streaks of green in it. The stem, or midrib, is the key to whether a leaf is dry or not. Never attempt to cure tobacco leaves with green stems.

I always use my garage for drying tobacco. The two doors are left open daily, producing the required current of air, and only closed at night when the atmosphere becomes damp. The direct rays of the sun *never* touch the tobacco.

Indeed, garages are ideal for drying provided that the leaves are hung high enough so that they do not become damaged by vehicles or persons.

The next step is the actual stringing up of the leaves. There are four methods:—

1 **A length of very thin wire** is attached to a hook in one wall, leaves are fed on to the line by means of pushing the rib ends on to the wire. When the line is full it is pulled taut, and the other end tied to a hook on the wall opposite the first.

2 **Long thin canes** are used, a knitting needle being used to make a hole in the rib ends for leaves to be threaded on to the canes.

3 **Twine is used,** the method of stringing up the leaves being the same as in 2.

4 **Leaves are hung up on hooks** in 'hands', (40 leaves), tied together at the rib ends.

I *always* use method 1. It is quick and easy, and one does not have to waste time piercing the rib end of each leaf, and then threading it. Actually, there is little to choose between methods 1—3 except for this. Method 4 I would discount altogether. The leaves are bunched too tightly, and the air cannot circulate amongst them to dry them. Long after leaves should have been dried off they will still be moist and green, and this is an open invitation to mildew.

There is one other method which I merely mention but would not advise. I learnt this from a man who had grown and cured his own leaf since the Kaiser's War. Once his leaf was harvested he used to lay it on a stone

40

floor and cover it with hessian sacks, weighed down with bricks. He always referred to this as 'fermentation', but having once sampled a pipe of his mixture I came to the conclusion that he was quite happy to smoke rotten leaf!

Therefore, having decided upon the wire method, we can begin. Leaves should be spaced at least six inches apart, with no more than twenty-five to a line. One is inclined to forget that freshly harvested tobacco leaf weighs heavy. I have had more than one wire snap in the past through overloading.

There is another tip which is worth noting. Always push your leaves on to the wire with each one facing alternately front to back. This is done because as the leaves dry, and they become lighter in weight, they are inclined to slide into each other, blown together by the constant current of air. By stringing them up in this way it means that they do not fit snugly together, and there is still room for the air to circulate between them.

Once each wire is pulled taut up towards the rafters, inspect the leaves, and make sure that they have not closed their gaps during this process.

For a whole month you will be fixing up more wires as you continue your harvest. I usually harvest at twice weekly intervals after the first gathering. This means that mature leaves are not left on the plants for longer than necessary, and are given every opportunity to dry out before the climate becomes damper.

It is a mistake to neglect the leaves that are drying. They must be watched constantly until it is time to take them down for curing, but the less you handle them the better. After the first ten days they will begin to furl and shrivel. Do not attempt to straighten them out because you will only damage them.

They will collect a variety of insects. Spiders love to spin their webs between the leaves. Also wasps are attracted to the curled leaves as places of warmth and comfort in which to hibernate for the coming winter. Consequently, it pays you to take care when finally it is time to remove the leaf from the wire for curing. I was once stung by a wasp during this process.

By the middle of September your leaf will be in varying stages of drying. That which you picked during the first week in August should now be ready for curing whilst the very last batch will only just be beginning to lose its lush green.

You can, if you wish, take down that which is ready, and begin curing it. Basically, it all depends upon what scale you are growing tobacco. If you are content to grow and smoke from year to year, then it will be advisable to wait until all your leaf is ready, and complete the process in a few days. If you are merely stockpiling, growing far more than you require for immediate smoking, then you will be curing throughout the winter months, and will probably be eager to start as soon as possible.

The aim of all home-tobacco enthusiasts is to build up a stock. Once leaf is properly dried, if stored in a cool dry place it will keep indefinitely. A friend of mine is at present curing leaf which he grew seven years ago. He still grows the same quantity each year, and eventually the day will arrive when he need grow no more. He will have a lifetime's supply.

STORING DRIED LEAF

If you are fortunate enough to grow more than your annual requirements, then care must be taken in storage. It is bad enough to lose drying leaf through mildew, but to lose it after you have overcome all the elementary problems is sheer waste of time and labour.

Smooth the leaves out, and store them flat, alternately front to back, in a cardboard carton. On no account use an airtight container or polythene bag. It is best to put no more than fifty leaves to a box, because if for some reason something does go wrong with a particular batch of leaf then your loss will be relatively small.

Attics are ideal for leaf storage provided they are weatherproof. Furthermore, you must inspect your stock from time to time. Once a month should be sufficient, and a note in your diary to that effect will ensure that you do not forget.

MILDEW

Mildew is your main enemy throughout the whole process of drying tobacco leaf. From the first week you hang your crop up in the garage to the time you take it down for curing, the leaf is vulnerable.

You cannot fail to spot mildew. Indeed, an experienced grower will smell it in the pleasant leafy aroma which fills your garage. It has a sharp pungent scent akin to the fermentation in home-made wine.

If you are lucky enough to spot mildew in its very early stages, with perhaps only one or two leaves carrying it, then remove them at once. It might be due to one or two inferior leaves that should not have been harvested. Yellowing leaves which have already started to decompose on the growing plant should never be hung up with good leaf. It is inviting disease. The compost heap is the only safe place for sub-standard leaf.

However, you may be unfortunate enough to discover that a large percentage of your leaf has mildew. You cannot afford to throw such a quantity away, and therefore you must attempt to combat it.

Spray your whole drying crop with a solution of one ounce of nitre to a gallon of water, or with a mixture of one ounce of flowers of sulphur to two gallons of soapy water. This should remove the mildew fairly quickly, but it may be necessary to spray more than once.

In all cases try to determine the cause of the mildew. Mostly it is caused either by the garage doors being left open on damp nights or else remaining closed during the daytime.

Weather-forecasting

Uncured tobacco leaf hanging in an airy place is a good guide to the weather which we can expect during the following twelve hours. Sea-weed can be put to a similar use.

When the leaf is damp we are likely to have rain or mist. Dry leaf means dry weather. However, in order to obtain some degree of accuracy the 'reading' should be taken in the middle of the day. Otherwise we are liable to misinterpret the dampness of early morning or evening as a sign of inclement weather to follow.

CURING IS NEXT STAGE

The leaf is dry and ready for curing. Now comes the most difficult part of all, an attempt to imitate the finished product of the large tobacco combines.

Firstly, though, the intention is to take a look at the equipment which is required to make the best of the nine months of 'toil'.

Figure 8 The Press.

CHAPTER 5

Equipment for Curing and Processing

The basic equipment needed for the curing and processing of a smokeable tobacco is as follows:—

1 **A large saucepan.** Rather than improvising with a kitchen cast-off, a new one, kept solely for the purpose of boiling tobacco is a good investment. The bigger the better. It will last for years.

2 **A press.** It is important to make blocks of tobacco for even shredding.

3 **Glass storage jars.** Again, as large as possible. The glass should be clear. Empty opaque coffee jars are inadvisable as it is difficult to keep an eye on the tobacco and spot mould in time to prevent a substantial loss.

4 **Flat 1 lb tobacco tins.** Most tobacconists who sell loose tobacco will be only too glad to give you these. They are useful for storing blocks of tobacco for a couple of days whilst they dry out prior to shredding. They also prevent the blocks from unfurling if packed tightly.

The *ingredients* necessary for curing will be dealt with in the section devoted to 'Curing and Processing'.

MAKING A PRESS

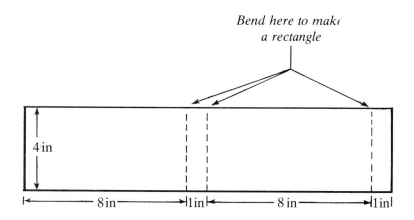

Bend here to make a rectangle

4 in

|← 8 in →|1in|← 8 in →|1in|

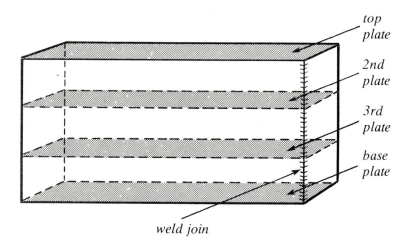

top plate

2nd plate

3rd plate

base plate

weld join

Diagram 5.1A Body of Press
(see Figure 11 for Finished Press)

THE PRESS
(see illustrations)

The press is **a simple construction made from mild steel capable of putting the maximum amount of pressure on the tobacco.** It should be capable of making at least three blocks at a time.

Leaf is pushed down to the bottom as tightly as is possible by hand, and then a plate dropped over it. The second and third processes are identical until the interior is filled with tobacco. The clamps may then be turned both at the same time so that even pressure is put on the tobacco. It is advisable that this stage is carried out in the sink for nicotine, and the mixture in which the leaves have been boiled, will ooze out in a sticky morass.

When the clamps will turn no more, leave them on full pressure for a few minutes, and then slowly loosen them. You should then be able to remove three blocks of dark moist tobacco which are immediately placed in one of the flat tins, and left there to dry out a little before shredding.

There is little to go wrong in this process, and if the novice is not satisfied with the finished product then he can always put the tobacco back in the press, and try again.

Nowadays, as far as I know, tobacco presses for the amateur are not manufactured commercially. Sometimes they can be obtained second-hand if you happen to know of someone who has given up the hobby. An advertisement in a local paper or *Exchange and Mart* is always worth a try, but in the event of this proving unsuccessful then you will either have to make

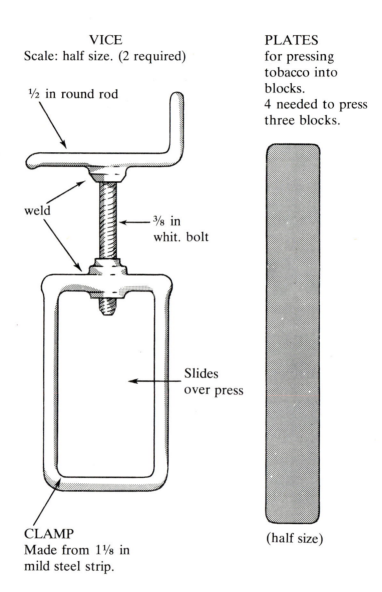

VICE
Scale: half size. (2 required)

½ in round rod

weld

⅜ in
whit. bolt

Slides
over press

CLAMP
Made from 1⅛ in
mild steel strip.

PLATES
for pressing
tobacco into
blocks.
4 needed to press
three blocks.

(half size)

Diagram 5.1B Side pieces and Plates for Press

one yourself or contact somebody who will do it for you. Overleaf is given a simple plan for the making of a tobacco-press which should prove sufficient for the needs of the average home-grower.

The chamber of the press is made from ⅛ in mild steel plate, welded into a box section down one edge. The base plates are also made of the same substance. All that is needed to manufacture your press is a vice, a hacksaw, and access to welding gear.

Although presses were formerly made of cast iron these are more easily made from mild steel and are equally as effective.

THE SHREDDER
(see illustrations)

The tobacco shredder **is similar in many ways to the average household mincing-machine.** A spindle drives the block of tobacco towards the knife, and the shredded tobacco falls on to a newspaper beneath. The principle is simple enough, but there are several snags which can arise and cause frustration to the user.

The machine should be well-greased with vaseline before use to enable it to work smoothly. **Never use oil or any other lubricant** for it will flavour the tobacco and make it unsmokeable.

Now, the chamber of your shredder should be roughly the same dimensions as the blocks of tobacco which your press makes. Some experience is necessary in the making of these blocks to achieve this, and in the early stages you may need to trim your pressed tobacco with a sharp knife in order to make it fit comfortably into the

51   *Continued on page 55*

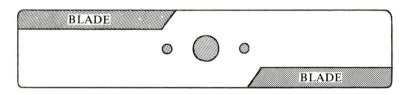

Double bladed knife for pipe cut
(Actual size)

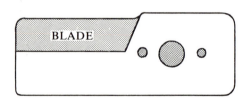

Single blade for cigarette cut
(Actual size)

Diagram 5.2A Making a Shredder—I (Blades)

Nut separating blade and handle

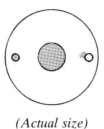

(Actual size)

TOBACCO RAM

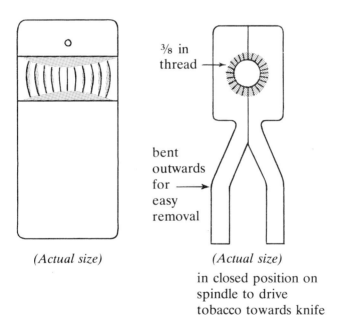

⅜ in thread →

bent outwards for → easy removal

(Actual size)   *(Actual size)*

in closed position on
spindle to drive
tobacco towards knife

Diagram 5.2B Making a Shredder—II
(Separating Nut and Shredder)

53

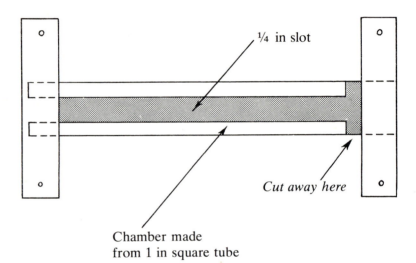

¼ in slot

Cut away here

Chamber made
from 1 in square tube

Diagram not in proportion

Diagram 5.2C Making a Shredder III
(Basic Structure of Shredder)

shredder.

If the block is too small it will not make much difference except that you have to do the same amount of work for less tobacco. But if the block is too large you may jam your shredder, and have to take the whole contraption to pieces and start all over again.

The blade is the most important feature for this determines the 'cut' of the tobacco, and as every smoker knows, this is vital to the quality of the smoke.

A *rough* cut smokes slowly, and is far cooler. This is ideal for a pipe, but only the individual smoker knows what suits him best.

A fine cut tobacco burns quickly, and smokes hot. Ideally this is a cigarette tobacco.

To obtain a coarse cut tobacco it is necessary to use only a single blade, but a double blade will produce your cigarette cut, simply by the processes of *two* cuts to *one* turn of the handle.

As in the case of the press you may experience difficulty in obtaining a shredder. If all else fails then here are some simple instructions for making one for yourself.

MAKING A SHREDDER

The shredder is also easily made from ⅛ in mild steel plate, and all that is needed is a vice, hacksaw, electric drill, a file, and, of course, access to welding gear. The blade, too, can be made from mild steel, and sharpened to a fine edge that will last for many shredding sessions. *(See diagrams).*

If you find that shredding is becoming hard work then

55 *Continued on page 58*

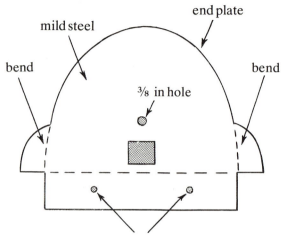

end plate

mild steel

bend   bend

³/₈ in hole

³/₁₆ in holes for fixing to bench

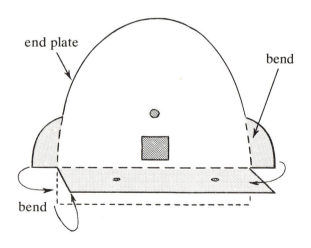

end plate

bend

bend

Diagram 5.2D Making a Shredder IV
(End Plates)

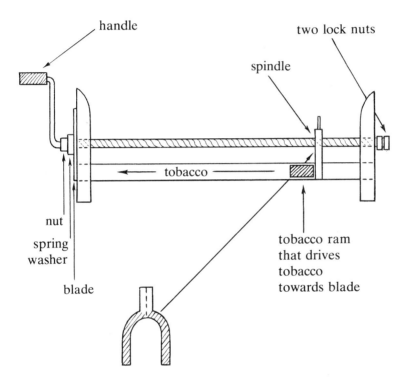

Diagram 5.2E Making a Shredder V
(assembled Shredder)

it is obvious that your machine is not functioning properly. There may be a variety of reasons for this. Perhaps your block of tobacco is too large for the shredder and is jamming it. More likely your blade is becoming blunt, and is not slicing through the moist tobacco as easily as it should. It is well worthwhile spending a few minutes sharpening your blade before each shredding session. Likewise, always ensure that your shredder is screwed securely to a firm surface. The lady of the house will probably object to having screws in the kitchen table so a large piece of four-ply is ideal, clamped to the table with a vice.

Always ensure that your shredder is empty before inserting a new block of tobacco. Lumps of leaf are apt to remain behind and clog the action.

ELIMINATE WASTAGE

There is always wastage during shredding. The last cut of a block seldom shreds properly, and a piece of tobacco about the size of your thumbnail falls on to the pile of shredded tobacco. Separate these lumps, and keep them on one side until the end. You will often find that you have sufficient to make an extra block from these bits, a gain of perhaps two ounces!

At all costs one has to eliminate waste. You may think that you have more than enough tobacco immediately following your harvest, but by the time it has dried, the mid-ribs have been removed, and you have cured it, you will be surprised just how little you have left at the end. The principle of growing your own, apart from the satisfaction gained, is to save money. So every bit of leaf you salvage during the final stages will be geared towards that end.

CHAPTER 6

Curing and Processing

TAKING DOWN THE DRIED LEAF

Now comes the most important stage of all. Many novice home-growers have lost their enthusiasm through being unable to achieve the ultimate in their season's work. Seedlings and plants have been nurtured for months, a battle against mildew has been fought and won, and then one falls at the very last hurdle. This is the reason why so many growers have discontinued. It is my hope that this book will help the first-time grower to be at least reasonably successful with his curing, and thereby encourage him to try again the following year. Like everything else in life, one learns by experience, and can only improve over the years. There is no reason, though, why you should not produce a smokeable product at the first attempt.

An inspection of your leaves will tell you whether or not they are ready to cure. You must be certain that they have dried off properly, though, otherwise you are doomed to failure. Unless the mid-ribs are dry, the tobacco will not cure.

If the leaf shows signs of being brittle, and crumbles to the touch, do not attempt to remove it from the wires.

Instead, leave your garage open overnight, and the atmosphere will dampen the tobacco sufficiently. Remove your leaves first thing in the morning before they become brittle again. It may be as well to plan your curing for a weekend in this case so that you can make an early start on either Friday or Saturday morning.

REMOVING THE MID RIBS

The first step, having taken your leaves off the wires, is to remove the mid-ribs. Stalk is unpleasant to smoke at the best of times, and judging from some of the cheaper commercial brands which I have tried, even the major tobacco companies do not always remove this.

Now there is a very quick and easy method of removing the stalk. I have watched growers painstakingly cutting them out with scissors. I can do ten to their one. Grip the end of the mid-rib with the thumb and forefinger of one hand, and then slide the thumb and forefinger of the other swiftly up the stalk. Leaf and mid-rib will separate perfectly.

It will certainly improve the quality of your smoke to have no stalk, whatsoever, in it, enabling the tobacco to draw evenly with the spontaneity of a cigar.

The time taken to prepare your leaf for the 'boiling' depends upon the amount which you have for curing. Lay the leaves out in batches, each one sufficient to fill your saucepan to capacity. Do not cram and overload as this will result in some of the leaf being improperly cured at the end. **You are now ready to start!**

Figure 9 Removal of Mid-rib.
Slide the leaf off the rib, holding the latter firmly
between finger and thumb.
Photo: Lance Smith

CURING AND PROCESSING

THE CURING 'MIXTURE'

The saucepan is filled with no more than an inch in depth of water which is brought to the boil. Once it begins to bubble you can make up your curing mixture by adding the following ingredients:—

2 tablespoonsfuls of BLACK TREACLE
2 - do - CLEAR HONEY
1 - do - BROWN SUGAR
1 - do - GLYCERIN
1 stick of LIQUORICE ROOT (usually one stick will do two or three boilings).

CURING

Stir well, and once the ingredients (with the exception of the stick of liquorice root) have dissolved, put your leaf in the saucepan, poke it well down, and then put the lid on. Allow it to boil for about ten minutes, and then let it simmer for the rest of the time. Always aim at one hour for each boiling. You have only to remove the lid and smell the rich vapour to realise exactly what is going into your tobacco.

One of the commonest faults is to boil for too long, and then discover before the hour is up that you have boiled dry, and your lower leaves are a mass of burnt sticky goo. This is one reason why you must lift the lid every ten minutes or so, and inspect. If you think that the water in the bottom is becoming too low then boil a kettle, and add some more. However, this will weaken your mixture, and so you must allow the tobacco to simmer for a little longer, i.e. if with ten minutes left to completion you are forced to add more water then boil

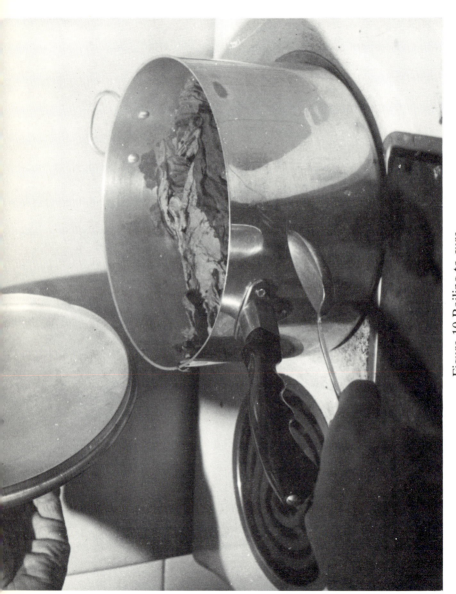

Figure 10 Boiling to cure.
Photo: Lance Smith

for a further ten minutes on top of the initial hour.

The hour is up, and it is time to take the cured leaf out of the saucepan. Tip it into the sink, and allow it to cool for five minutes. Whilst you are waiting for this, prepare your next lot of mixture, and put another batch of leaves on to boil. You have now developed a sequence, and you will be kept busy for the rest of the day.

PRESSING

Once the boiled leaf is sufficiently cool enough to handle, you can begin putting it in the press. It is advisable to do this in the sink also as the tobacco will ooze mixture and nicotine throughout the operation. There is no need to try and separate the leaves. Part a few from the main bunch, approximately enough to make one block, and poke them down into the bottom of the press, laying them as evenly as possible before dropping the first steel plate on top of them.

Three sticky blocks are in the press, and now you begin to turn the two clamps until they are at full pressure. Leave them like this for ten minutes or so, during which time you can check that boiling number two is progressing satisfactorily.

To remove your blocks of tobacco from the press, unscrew the clamps and press down on the top plate. All three should fall out fairly easily.

The block tobacco should now look dark and wholesome. Waste no time in transferring it to the flat 1 lb tobacco tins because once it begins to dry it will unfurl, and make shredding all the more difficult.

Figure 11 Pressing.

Blocks of tobacco just removed from the press. These will be shaped

FLAVOURING

This is a matter purely for individual taste. The flavouring of high grade tobacco is achieved by the blending of different varieties of leaf. However, the choice of the home-grower is somewhat limited so if a strong flavour is desired (often it is used to disguise bad leaf) then one must take great care. It would be terrible, indeed, to render the tobacco unsmokeable at this stage!

Ten years or so ago it was possible to purchase flavourings from the company who were then chemists to the tobacco industry. I bought two varieties. 'Warwick Flake' was designed for a darker tobacco, whilst 'New Mown Hay' was suitable for cigarette tobacco. It is necessary to use no more than half a teaspoonful per boiling, and even this fills the house with a pungent aroma which lasts for at least a week! In my opinion it makes tobacco too piquant, although if the jars are allowed to mature for about a year or more the flavour becomes reasonable subtle.

I still have more than half of both bottles intact on top of the kitchen cupboard, and it may be that one day I shall decide to experiment with them again.

Some cake flavourings, obtainable from most chemists' shops, are equally as good, particularly *Vanilla*. However, it is as well to experiment on a small boiling of leaves before making a choice in this matter. The flavourings do not always smell the same in cured tobacco as they do in their bottles.

SHREDDING

The following day your blocks of tobacco should be

Figure 12 Shredding blocks of tobacco
Photo: Lance Smith

dry enough for shredding. If you discover that they are too moist, which makes cutting decidedly laborious, then leave them another day. No longer, though, because mould can start even at this early stage.

Having shredded your blocks in the manner described earlier in this book, you are now ready for the next stage.

TOASTING

This is a vital process which is all too often neglected by home-growers. It serves two purposes. Firstly, it completes the drying-off of your tobacco, thereby guarding against mould, and secondly it gives your finished product a rich golden appearance, a really professional touch.

For this you will require a grill on moderate heat, and a kitchen fork. Spread a handful of shredded tobacco in the grill-pan sparingly.If you fill it too deeply some of the leaf will escape the heat altogether.

Under no circumstances put your tobacco under the grill and leave it. You must watch it at all times, pulling the pan out, and teasing it with the fork every few seconds. Here you will learn by trial and error. You must not burn the tobacco or dry it too much. Your aim is to leave a certain amount of moistness in it, approximately that to be found in a newly opened airtight tin of commercial tobacco. Use this as a guide.

If you discover that you have dried some of it too much, then lay it out on a newspaper in your garage overnight, leaving the doors open. The moisture content will have returned by morning.

Do not put your toasted tobacco immediately into

Figure 13 Toasting shredded tobacco.
Photo: Lance Smith

containers. I always lay mine spread out evenly on newspapers overnight, and then inspect it again the following morning. Invariably some needs re-toasting for no matter how careful you are, you are always likely to miss some.

CONTAINERS

As I have stated before, always use *clear* glass containers so that you can spot any mould early on. Empty sweet jars are ideal if you can persuade your local shop to part with them.

Do not pack the tobacco tightly. Rather, fill the jars lightly without pressing the leaf down, and for the first week at least **leave the lids off.**

Tobacco at this stage is best stored in a cool dry place.

When inspecting your jars daily do not forget to examine the bottoms for this is a favourite place for mould to start. Smell them too. Any drastic change in aroma means that something is wrong.

After the first week it is generally safe to screw the lids on the jars, but you must continue to keep an eye on the tobacco for the first month or so. Mould is not always in a hurry to show itself.

MOULD

In the event of spotting mould, remove the infected area at once. You may be lucky and lose only a couple of pipefuls, or it may mean throwing away an ounce or more. If you do not do this you will most certainly lose the whole jar.

Mould is almost always caused by a high moisture

Figure 14 The finished product ready for smoking.
Photo: Lance Smith

content. You probably have not toasted your leaf enough, but it is too late to rectify this now. The safest way is to tip out the jar in which you have discovered the mould, and dry it off thoroughly in front of a fire or a central-heating radiator. Electric fires are inclined to give off heat that is too dry, and you may find yourself having to leave the tobacco in the garage again for it to re-absorb moisture. In any case, at the first sign of mould, step up your vigilance.

WHEN TOBACCO IS READY FOR SMOKING

Tobacco, like wine, improves with keeping. The ideal situation to reach is one in which you smoke the leaf which you cured the previous year. However, the grower who achieves this is generally the exception rather than the rule.

It would be foolish and wasteful to begin smoking your leaf immediately after curing. In fact, the tobacco would smoke so hot that it would be an unpleasant experience, and the novice would probably decide that all the effort was not worth the end product.

Do not be in a hurry even to sample your tobacco until at least a month has passed since it was put into the containers. By the following January it should be maturing nicely, and this is the earliest I would advocate to begin smoking it.

BLENDING

Only you can decide whether or not your tobacco is of sufficient quality to smoke entirely on its own. The process I have described is designed to add *body* to the leaf. Without this it is insipid and flavourless.

However, many growers blend their tobacco with commercial brands, and if one is prepared to experiment properly, the one will complement the other. If you blend on a fifty-fifty proportion you are cutting your previous smoking costs by half, and enjoying the best of both worlds. You will add to the nicotine content, although even this will be halved when compared with the average smoker who buys all his tobacco.

Blending is an art all of its own, in just the same way as the growing and curing of leaf. There are many tobacconists throughout the country who blend and sell their own brands simply by buying different varieties of leaf, and knowing exactly which one complements another.

Bad blending can produce an unpleasant smoke from two varieties which are excellent when used on their own.

The ideal way to experiment with blending is to start with small quantities. Favour the brand which you used to smoke before you became involved in the hobby. Try an ounce of it mixed with an identical quantity of your home-grown. If you decide you like it, all well and good, otherwise try something else.

Specialist tobacconists sell blending tobaccos, i.e. tobaccos which are not suitable for smoking on their own, but require the addition of another leaf. There are fastidious smokers who prefer to buy and blend their own, even rather than purchase a mixture from a well-known blender. They are connoisseurs, men to whom pipe-smoking is an art rather than an addiction. So, it is necessary to learn something about basic tobacco blending:—

Latakia is a jet black leaf that mostly comes from Syria. It has been cured by a slow process of being hung over smouldering oak fires. Its aroma is distinctive, easily recognisable anywhere, and it is used in a large proportion of high quality smoking mixtures. Above all, it smokes cool, has a delightful eastern flavour about it, and enhances most tobaccos with which it is blended. Personally, I would never consider blending without Latakia.

Cavendish is another black tobacco, but less subtle in its flavour. In many ways it is reminiscent of a mild form of 'twist'. It adds body to any mixture, and helps to slow down any tobacco that is inclined to smoke swiftly. When one smells Cavendish before it is blended it may seem to be rather harsh, but this disappears once it is mixed with another variety.

Turkish tobacco we are all familiar with from the days when those oval shaped cigarettes used to command great popularity. The coarser cut for pipes has a less pungent aroma, and bears a similarity to Latakia. It is often blended with Latakia.

Virginia. Possibly the finest of all tobaccos whether used in pipe or cigarette manufacture. Nowadays Virginia is used primarily as a blending tobacco as the cost of pure Virginia is beyond the purse of the average smoker. It comes in many forms, dark, light, fine and coarse.

I have my own favourite blend, and in this I use expensive tobaccos because I am smoking them at half-cost, anyway. Now that I have tried and perfected my blend I usually mix up a couple of pounds at a time in the following proportions:—

1 lb of Home Cured Tobacco.

2 oz Latakia (this is best used sparingly, otherwise it is inclined to dominate a mixture).

4 oz. Cavendish.

2 oz. Light Virginia.

8 oz. My favourite commercial brand.

Here is an important tip once you have become reasonably experienced in curing and blending. **Mould is less likely to plague home-grown tobacco once blending tobaccos have been added.** I discovered this some years ago when mould started to form in every jar *except* those to which blending tobaccos had been added. Consequently, in the years that followed, once my cured leaf has undergone a few weeks in the jars I blend it all up. This requires an outlay of some £20, mostly spent on Latakia and Cavendish with the other varieties being added at a later stage.

It is an interesting point that **home-grown leaf will absorb the flavour of any tobacco with which it is mixed.** So, if you just want to smoke your favourite tobacco at a reduced cost, mix it in equal proportions with your own.

SMOKING WITHOUT BLENDING

Of course, there are many home-growers who consider that their leaf produces a satisfying smoke without the addition of any blending tobaccos. The only snag is that most of us have been brought up on commercial brands, and find it hard to get away from them.

If you decide that you simply wish to smoke that which you have grown and cured yourself, then I can only compliment you upon your efforts. However, you may find that the addition of glycerin into the finished product adds that little extra.

Glycerin is something else which adds body. The only way of applying it to shredded leaf is to spread your tobacco out on newspapers, pour glycerin on to your hands, and then rub it into the tobacco. It is messy, but effective.

Glycerin is also a mould-repellant. I always include it in my boiling mixture for this reason. Glycerin is also one of the best 'revitalisers' of stale tobacco. Some time ago a friend of mine visited one of those old-fashioned tobacconists' shops which was holding a 'closing-down' sale due to the death of the proprietor. The assistant happened to mention that they still had some packets of pre-war flake tobaccos down in the cellar.

My friend was not slow to offer to dispose of it for her, and came away with several ounces of a well-known brand in the original packets. The tobacco resembled blocks of wood, the flakes completely inseparable.

However, within a matter of hours glycerin had restored the tobacco to its original condition. The dark juicy tobacco was rubbed out, then blended with his home-grown leaf, and I can personally vouch for the quality of a superb smoke.

CIGAR MAKING

The making of cigars from your own tobacco requires more than a little experience. Firstly, to obtain the best

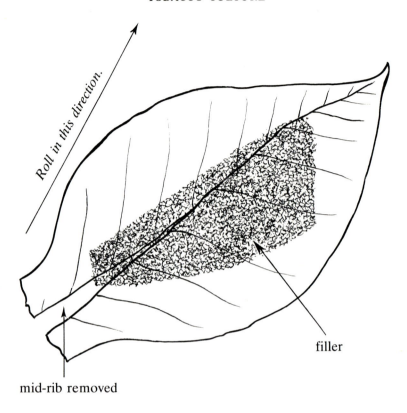

Roll in this direction.

mid-rib removed

filler

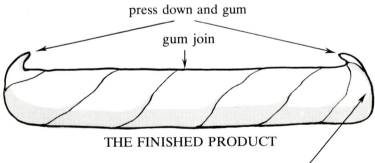

press down and gum

gum join

THE FINISHED PRODUCT

pierce several small holes with a pin prior to smoking.

Diagram 6.1 Essentials of cigar-making.

results you must grow a few Hungarian leaves for use as outer-wrappers, and some Havana for the filler. Brazilian is a good substitute if you merely want to try your hand during the main task of producing pipe or cigarette tobacco.

The leaf has to be dried in exactly the same manner as described, and the mid-ribs removed for easy rolling. Place the wrapper leaf on a flat surface with the filler positioned diagonally across it for that is the direction in which you are going to attempt to roll your cigar.

Roll it in the same way that you would hand-roll a cigarette. It is a knack which either you will develop or you won't. No amount of instruction will turn you into a good cigar-maker.

Once you have achieved a fairly cylindrical shape, use some ordinary clear gum to hold the leaf in place before it unfurls. Bend both ends over, and gum them down, too. Well, at least you have made a cigar of some sort, but do not make the mistake of smoking it right away.

Cigars are best stored in cedar-wood boxes. Perhaps your tobacconist will be only too pleased to get rid of a few. I would advise storing the boxes in a room where the temperature seldom drops below 60°F, and do not smoke the cigars for at least six months.

Cigar-making is one more step towards economy. During the process of removing the mid-ribs from your leaves you cannot avoid crumbling some of the leaves which are drier than the rest. Use these bits as filler for your cigars rather than throw them away. Everything you do to eliminate waste helps to keep the rapidly devaluing pound in your pocket.

space for cigar

wooden blocks

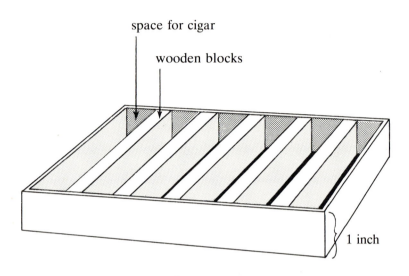

1 inch

Cigars can be moulded by the use of a wooden box with blocks at intervals of 1½ inches. Roll your cigar in the manner of a cigarette, but ensure that the lid of the box fits tightly. Shape and regularity is more easily gained in this way.

Diagram 6.2 Alternative method of cigar-making.

CIGARETTES

Cigarette tobacco must draw evenly at all times. A pipe smoker does not mind relighting his briar on a number of occasions, but there is nothing more annoying than the cigarette which constantly goes out. This is due to one of two reasons: (a) damp tobacco (b) uneven distribution of the leaf in the cigarette.

When toasting your tobacco for cigarettes always endeavour to see that it is comparatively dry. This is the stage at which to control your moisture-content.

Do not pack the tobacco tightly into the cigarette paper. Pull the shreds apart by hand, and then pack them into the paper, ensuring that the air can pass through. It is a good idea, health reasons apart, to use a filter-tip. This facilitates drawing, and also prevents shreds of tobacco from getting into your mouth. If you are 'learning' to roll cigarettes entirely by hand it will help you to form an even cylinder.

Hand rolling without the aid of a machine is an art which it may take some time to accomplish. Shape the paper first, lie it on a flat surface, and pack in the tobacco until it is just full enough for the two ends to meet comfortably. Roll it between your fingers lightly to shape it, and then stick it down. Allow a couple of seconds or so for the gum to stick properly. Perseverance may be necessary before you are fully satisfied. Do not try to match the skill of the western cowboy who rolls his smokes one-handed whilst riding his horse!

The Origin of Cigarette Rolling

Rumour has it that the first cigarette was rolled by an

Egyptian gunner at the siege of Acre in 1832. Having lost his clay pipe, and craving for a smoke, he decided to try rolling his tobacco in the paper of spent cartridges. Little did he realise that he had invented the first cigarette! Other soldiers followed his example, making their cigarettes from a variety of materials including rags, pages from books, and even dried leaves.

As the smoking of tobacco in this way grew in popularity, the manufacture of cigarette papers began towards the latter end of the nineteenth century. Because of their texture and appearance they became known as rice paper. Cigarette smoking was here to stay in spite of the disapproval of Queen Victoria.

Rizla

And now a few words about the Rizla Company which has made cigarette rolling so easy for thousands of smokers.

Rizla's origins were with Citizen LaCroix, who was granted a licence to manufacture fine paper on the 18th April, 1799 in France, although the company's paper-making history goes back as far as the mid-seventeenth century. For the next half century L. LaCroix Fils of Angouleme continued to produce general papers. The name Rizla was derived from the French word for rice (riz), combined with a visual pun on the LaCroix name, croix being French for cross, to produce Riz La +. This was eventually shortened to "Rizla", a name that has been part of the English tradition since the late nineteenth century. With factories in France, Belgium, Canada, and Australia, associates in Benelux, and distributors all over the world, Rizla is now the largest producer of cigarette papers in the world. The original French parent company is now a subsidiary to the headquarters in Treforest.

The popularity of handrolling today

Sales of handrolling tobacco and cigarette papers grew dramatically during World War II, and reached its peak around 1964. It would appear that the number of smokers who roll their own is strongly influenced by the economic climate, and increases in price of tailormade cigarettes always provide an upsurge in the sales of handrolling materials. During 1969 and 1971 there were few increases in the price of tailormade cigarettes so they became relatively cheaper in terms of customer expenditure, and the sales of handrolling tobacco declined slightly. From 1972 to 1974 the handrolling market remained virtually static. However, in 1974 handrolling was the only sector of tobacco goods which increased sales by weight, so it would seem that the duty and price increases of 1974 and 1975 have caused a revival in growth of handroller figures. The latest figures show that in 1975 14.2 million lbs. manufactured weight of tobacco was sold to the public in the U.K. an increase of 700,000 lbs. on 1974.

It is estimated that approximately 2 million men and 200,000 women roll a total of approximately 10,000 million cigarettes per year. The majority of handrollers are outdoor workers, but during the past two or three years a great proportion of students and under-25 year-

Figure 15 Cigarette Papers
(Courtesy: Rizla Ltd.)

olds are turning to rolling, indicating a marked preference for the fresher and more individualistic taste of handrolled tobacco.

We can see clearly, therefore, the advantages of hand-rolling cigarettes. Yet, these advantages are doubled when home-cured tobacco is used. The cost will be fractional, the effects far less harmful, but overall will be the constant feeling of satisfaction at having made a cigarette, possibly from tobacco grown from seed.

In order to assist the smoker in his choice of handrolling materials we list below the Rizla products and accessories:—

RIZLA PRODUCTS*
Papers

Rizla **red** and **green** papers have similar medium burning qualities, the only difference being that the green papers have cut corners to facilitate entry into rolling machines. The single booklets contain 100 leaves, and are packed in boxes of 100. Double booklets are packed in 25s. **Red** papers are also available as a King size paper, packed in boxes of 50 booklets.

Liquorice papers, packed in boxes of 50 booklets are heavily coated papers with a high degree of water resistance. The pleasant liquorice flavour has been a favourite for many years.

Rizla **Wheetstraw** is made from natural straw fibres, and burns and tastes differently to any other paper in the range. Double Wheetstraw are packed in 25s, king size in 50s.

Details by courtesy of Rizla Ltd.

RIZLA LUXURY

MINI–MAXI

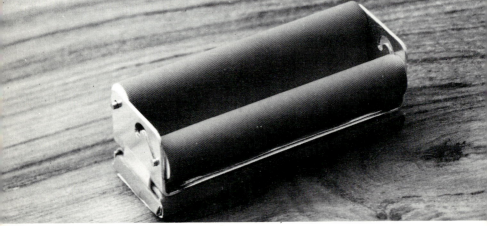

CADET

Figure 16 Cigarette-making Machines Reduced in size. *(Courtesy: Rizla Ltd.)*

Machines

The **Cadet** machine has been produced for many years and the company still sell one million annually. The **Mini-Maxi** machine was introduced in 1973. Available in red, blue or black, this sturdy little machine has the unique facility of pre-determining the thickness of the cigarette to be rolled by the flick of a switch.

Rizla's **Luxury** machine is a sophisticated version of the mini-maxi, beautifully finished in brushed aluminium. Attractive and compact for a lady's handbag, and stylish enough for any boardroom.

The **Rizla Rolling Box** is the latest product. Approximately the size of a cigarette packet, one simply loads the box with paper and tobacco, closes the lid, and up pops a perfect cigarette. The Rolling Box is made from non-corroding stainless steel to keep tobacco fresh.

Accessories

Rizla Kits and pouches provide your own cigarette factory in your pocket.

The **Rizla Kit** is made from durable black plastic with a matt finish lid, and contains a mini-maxi machine, filter tips and papers. There is a compartment for tobacco.

Rizla **pouches** are made in three differently coloured tartans, black nylon and trendy blue denim. Each pouch contains a mini-maxi machine, filter tips and papers, with a separate waterproof insert for the tobacco.

ventilators

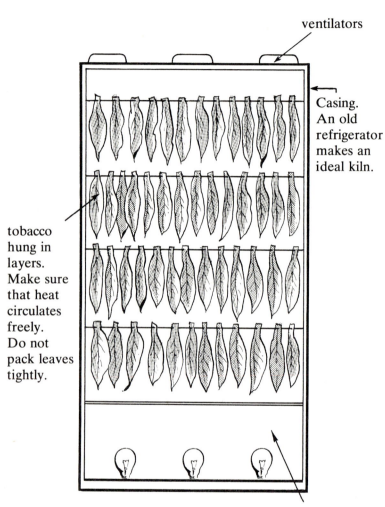

Casing.
An old
refrigerator
makes an
ideal kiln.

tobacco
hung in
layers.
Make sure
that heat
circulates
freely.
Do not
pack leaves
tightly.

Heating Unit.
Electric light bulbs
will provide the
heat necessary.

Diagram 6.3 Making a Tobacco Kiln for curing.

88

Rizla **Filter tips**—the final accessory for the discerning smoker.

OTHER CURING METHODS

There are several more ways of curing tobacco other than the one I have detailed. Most of them have been tried, discarded, and cast into obscurity.

Perhaps the 'flue' method is the only one really worthy of mention. This is really a kiln with a regulated heat in which the tobacco leaves are hung for some weeks. At the end of that time all that remains is for the leaf to be shredded. I have had my crop cured in this way on a couple of occasions, but, in my opinion, the result was very neutral, and I ended up by boiling the remainder of the leaves with my crop the following year.

Continental growers seem to disregard curing altogether, merely hanging their leaves in the eaves of their houses to dry, and then smoking the tobacco almost straight away.

I once knew a man who used a curing mixture very similar to my own . . . except that he did not apply it until *after* the tobacco had been shredded. Perhaps 'cut' would be more applicable than 'shredded' for he did not possess a shredder, refused the loan of mine, and preferred to use a pair of scissors. The mixture was applied with a small hair-spray. I once tried his tobacco. It was coarse, needless to say, required constant re-lighting, and both tasted and smelled unpleasant. Nevertheless, he lived until he was almost ninety!

I cannot leave out the method of 'twist' curing in a book of this nature. Actually, the tobacco leaves are not rolled up tightly in rope whilst thay are still green, as is fondly believed. They are dried in the usual manner, and then rolled. Naturally, it is a strong tobacco because the nicotine has been compressed in it rather than being extracted under normal curing processes. If you do not possess a press and shredder, and have no inclination either to buy, borrow, or make them, then no doubt this is the method for you. However, tobacco grown in Britain does not possess the 'strength' to produce a really effective twist.

I maintain, **and so do those who have sampled my tobacco, that the boiling method of curing is the only way in which a tobacco approaching professional standards can be achieved.** It is hard work, and messy, and you will no doubt incur the wrath of the lady of the house during that autumn spell when you dominate her kitchen, but in the end it will have its reward. Nothing worthwhile is ever accomplished easily.

One legal point that is worth noting is that if a friend approaches you with some leaf which he has grown, and is too lazy to cure it for himself, then there is nothing to stop you doing it for him . . . so long as you do not process it. Once you do that, you are contravening Customs and Excise regulations.

CHAPTER 7

General Smoking Hints

Having learnt how to produce a tobacco within the confines of one's own garden and house, perhaps a few general hints might assist the smoker in obtaining maximum pleasure from the weed. Mostly these will be directed at the pipe-smoker for some 80% of those who grow and cure their own tobacco consume it this way. Likewise, the inveterate cigarette-smoker who has shown sufficient interest in the cause of his addiction could well be deciding that perhaps the greater pleasure lies in a pipe after all.

CHOICE OF A PIPE

A cheap pipe is seldom a good buy. Admittedly, one finds the odd one which proves to be satisfactory over a length of time, but mostly they smoke hot, and spoil the flavour of the tobacco. On the other hand, a very expensive briar is often wasted on the average smoker. One has to strike a happy medium, and I would go for a good sound briar in the £3/£4 bracket.

Size and shape also require a certain amount of careful consideration. Do you like a large or small bowl? Do you prefer a bent or a straight stem?

Firstly, let me point out that a large pipe is more expensive to smoke than a small one. It sounds ridiculous, but it is a fact. One might think that one large pipe of tobacco is equivalent to two small ones. This is not so. As in the case of the man who prefers small cigarettes because half his pleasure is obtained by lighting another one, so the pipe-smoker enjoys filling his pipe, and getting it going. Large or small pipe, the number of smokes per day will vary little.

I generally prefer the ¾ oz briar. Small and light, it rests easily between the teeth at all times. The design is generally dictated by one's smoking habits. If you smoke whilst working, whether indoors or outdoors, you will need a pipe that is not cumbersome, and does not obstruct you. Likewise, the sportsman, the shooting man or the fisherman, will prefer a short or bent stem that is not likely to get in the way of rod or gun.

Smoking out-of-doors is less economical than smoking indoors. The tobacco burns much quicker, and if there is a strong wind one's smoking time per pipe may be reduced by as much as 50%.

The cut of tobacco, too, is influenced by whether you smoke inside or outside. Outdoor smokers are better with a slow burning, coarse cut tobacco. It is a good idea to mix plug or flake into your home-grown leaf in this case. Possibly a finer cut will suit the more leisurely indoor smoker.

BREAKING-IN A PIPE

Never smoke a new pipe out-of-doors until it is fully 'broken in'. Breaking-in consists of collecting an *even* lining of carbon on the inside of the bowl so that the wood does not burn, and cause an unpleasant flavour on the palate. Some pipes are manufactured with a carbonised bowl which eliminates the process as far as the smoker is concerned.

A pipe never smokes well during the breaking-in period. You will invariably taste the new wood from time to time, but you must persevere. It may take as many as thirty pipefuls of tobacco before you can enjoy a satisfying smoke.

When breaking-in a new pipe choose a time when you are most relaxed; i.e. watching television or reading. Only half-fill the bowl for your first smoke, pressing the tobacco down evenly, and ensuring that there are no lumps which will spoil the smooth burning of the leaf.

Do not be afraid of ample flame, and ensure that the whole of the top surface of the tobacco is alight. Uneven burning will mean that only part of the bowl is being carbonised. Likewise, do not be afraid to re-light your pipe time and time again if it goes out. This is something which new smokers must bear with.

Smoke the tobacco right through, and develop the habit of leaving as little 'dottle' (the unsmoked tobacco in the bottom of the bowl) as possible. It is wasteful, as well as causing an uneven distribution of carbon, to leave a large plug of tobacco unsmoked.

Allow your pipe to cool thoroughly in between smokes. For the second smoke fill the bowl three-quarters full, and on the third pack it almost to the top.

Many good pipes are totally ruined by unorthodox methods of breaking-in. Soaking the bowl with spirit

93

will produce an exceedingly hot and unpleasant smoke, and holding the pipe over a gas-jet is likely to do irreparable damage.

The only way to break-in a pipe is to smoke it in the way I have described.

DAMAGE TO PIPES

Many pipes are damaged by knocking the bowl on a hard surface in an attempt to dislodge a stubborn dottle. One of two things are liable to happen. The bowl will either crack or split, or else the stem will snap. There are a variety of smokers' knives on the market, obtainable from most tobacconists, nearly all of which incorporate a scraper. Use this to remove the dottle, and also when the carbon inside the bowl becomes too thick.

Too much carbon is liable to crack the bowl. I once witnessed this happen to an experienced smoker. There was a loud crack like the report of a cap-pistol, and half the bowl fell away, and deposited smouldering tobacco all over the unfortunate man's clothing.

Do not try and remove the carbon right down to the wood. You are risking cracking the bowl, and also you will have to go through the unpleasant process of building up the carbon again in order to obtain a mellow smoke.

CLEANING

A satisfying smoke cannot be obtained without regular cleaning. A pipe-cleaner should be used daily, and it is best to develop a routine, perhaps doing it last thing at night before retiring, and then leaving bowl and mouthpiece separated so that they dry thoroughly. If you have access to a regular supply of large poultry feathers these will serve admirably as pipe-cleaners. Methylated spirit is an ideal cleanser to use in conjunction with these. I have seen cold tea being used, too, but I do not think that it compares with the former. Most smokers possess more than one pipe. Several I know have one for each day of the week which is an excellent idea because it gives each briar six days rest in between smoking.

Pipes not in use are best stored in a pipe-rack, bowls downwards. This really gives them a chance to dry out. Make sure, though, that there are no dottles left in them as this will tend to sour them. Never, under any circumstance, leave a half-smoked pipe overnight, and then light it again the following morning. It is the equivalent of saving up all your dottles, and then smoking them!

SAFETY MEASURES

Fire hazard is something which we must guard against at all times. The carelessly tossed away cigarette-end is the most popular conception of how fires are started, but the risk from pipe smokers is just as great.

I once had an unnerving experience myself many years ago. I was wearing a nylon macintosh at the time, walking through a crowded provincial town, smoking my pipe. As I walked into a store I noticed a 'no smoking' sign and as my pipe appeared to have gone out, anyway, I put it in the pocket of my mac. Some ten minutes later I was back outside in the street when I detected a smell of burning. Some demolition work was in progress nearby, and my first reaction was that the unpleasant aroma was coming from a bonfire of old tarpaulins. Suddenly, I felt a tap on the shoulder.

"Hey, mister!" an alarmed elderly woman shouted, "You're on fire!"

I glanced down, and smoke was billowing up out of my smouldering pocket.

Fortunately, there happened to be a convenient puddle nearby, following a recent shower of rain, and without further ado I shed my smoking garment and doused it unceremoniously in the muddy water.

My loss was a cheap coat. It could have been far worse. **Never put a pipe in your pocket without first removing the remaining tobacco into a place of safety.**

Some people have an annoying and exceedingly dangerous habit of tapping out their pipes into the nearest waste-paper basket. This once happened in an office where I worked. Fortunately, the waste-paper basket happened to be a metal one, and the small bonfire was contained within it. The ashtray is the commonest item of furniture in the world, so use it!

DRY AND STALE TOBACCO

Particularly in hot weather, tobacco kept in anything other than an airtight container is apt to become dry very quickly. A dry smoke as such is unpleasant to the palate, and if you are only a very moderate smoker then it is best to carry only small amounts of tobacco in your pouch.

In the event of the tobacco becoming dry, though, there is no need to waste it. It can either be spread out

96

on a newspaper and left in an open garage or porch overnight, or else a slice of potato or apple can be placed in the pouch. Either of these methods quickly restores the leaf to its former condition.

Nowadays a national shortage of tins has led to many of the major tobacco companies resorting to other types of containers for their product. By far the best is the polythene pouch, and home-growers could do worse than beg a few of the empties from their friends. They keep tobacco much fresher than the conventional pouch.

SMOKING COMPETITIONS

During the last few years national pipe-smoking contests have been held, and it is interesting to note that competitors have kept very small quantities of tobacco alight for periods in excess of an hour and a half. Pipes and tobacco are provided by the organisers in order to eliminate unfair advantage.

These competitors are *real* pipe-smokers. If we could emulate them, our pleasure would be doubled at half the cost even when smoking home-grown leaf. This is the *art* of smoking. Puffing furiously merely brings about a hot, wet smoke. We must learn to draw with no more effort than it takes to breathe, savouring the delicate flavour of the leaf.

During the First World War the *Daily Mail* ran a campaign for people to produce their own tobacco, and a booklet was published on the subject. No prizes were offered other than the saving, and some satisfaction and pleasure during the darkest days.

The time is right for us to begin growing and curing again in earnest. This time the enemy is inflation and respiratory diseases. How long before the £1 ounce of tobacco? Surely, though, our health is even more important.

Old mottos are looming up again. **Dig, Grow and Cure for Victory!**

CHAPTER 8

A Short History of Tobacco

Tobacco had been smoked around the globe for centuries before it was discovered by the Europeans. It was first introduced to Europe about 1560 by Francisco Hernandez, a physician of Philip II of Spain who discovered it in Mexico. It was considered to be a panacea, a medicine that was a cure for all ills, contrary to modern belief that it is detrimental to the health, and it was only available in chemists' shops. We must remember, though, that the leaf was smoked in its pure form, mostly only dried with no attempts being made at curing, and had no tar content as is found in present day commercial tobaccos.

So, tobacco found its way to Europe, and it was here to stay. Tradition has it that Sir Walter Raleigh was the first man to smoke tobacco in England, and we have all read varying accounts of how a well-meaning colleague threw a pail of water over him, fully believing that Sir Walter was on fire. However, it is Captain Ralph Lane who is officially credited with being the first British smoker. The leaf in question was from the West Indies, collected by Christopher Columbus during an exploration of Cuba in 1492. Ralph Lane demonstrated the art of smoking to the English, but it was Sir Walter Raleigh who introduced it to society. It received a mixed reception.

Tobacco was very expensive and could only be smoked by the wealthy. There are varying reports concerning its price. In its infancy it could be purchased for its own weight in silver, and then, as it gained popularity, it commanded a price of something in the region of three shillings for four ounces. On this latter basis, inflation did not begin for three hundred years!

Parliament was soon to realise the revenue potential, and introduced an excise duty on *pipes* in 1644. Since 1620 pipe-making had been declared a London monopoly, and anybody else who sold pipes risked a fine in the region of twenty shillings.

Tobacco cultivation was forbidden by law in England in January 1631, and only London importation was permitted. However, this was withdrawn in 1639, possibly due to the fact that so much smuggling was taking place that it made a mockery of the law. Tobacco could from then onwards be imported at Bristol, Plymouth, Dartmouth and Southampton, a factor which considerably boosted local trade.

However, English grown tobacco was proving detrimental to the import trade, and it was soon clear that much revenue was being lost to home-grown leaf. The laws of 1631 were being flouted, and it was largely due to the ownership of English tobacco plantations by magistrates that nothing was being done about it. In 1652 the House of Commons passed a new law forbidding the cultivation of leaf and authorising *anyone* to destroy the plantations. This led to a series of riots and unrest throughout the country so Parliament resolved that a duty of threepence per lb. should be paid by all growers, but the concession was for one year only. No doubt it was hoped that this levy would ruin the 'home' trade, and that within twelve months the only tobacco being smoked would be imported leaf.

Yet, after that period was up, the growing continued as before. Home-growers might be interested to learn that the county of Gloucestershire was where the majority of leaf was grown. Possibly the climate there is more suited to tobacco-growing than anywhere else in this country. More likely, though, the reason is to be found in an abundance of magistrates who felt that by congregating in one county they stood a better chance of flouting the law.

Yet, the government was determined this time, and in June 1655 army officers in Gloucestershire, Somerset, and Bristol were ordered to destroy *all* tobacco plantations in those counties. However, the destruction of one year's crop did not mean an end to British tobacco-growing. Royalist plans for a revolution were nearing completion, and in the State Papers of 1656, addressed to Secretary Nicholas, the exiled King's Minister in Cologne, it was promised that if the King landed on English soil he could depend upon the support of some 600 malcontented tobacco planters from Gloucester.

During the following six years tobacco was still grown in England despite the efforts of the government to suppress it, and there is a report that in August 1662 the army was called out in Tormarton to destroy all tobacco growing in the Bristol area.

Annual government proclamations were issued prohibiting the growing of tobacco, but the culture went unchecked, much to the discontent of Bristol tobacco-merchants. Bristol was by now the leading tobacco port of England, and it was estimated that approximately half of the shipping unloaded was imported tobacco.

By 1670 smoking was an accepted practice, and was as common amongst women and schoolboys as it was amongst men! However, fashions come and go, and by the Restoration Era it had lost much of its popularity. Of course, up to then smoking was mostly confined to pipes, as it was until the outbreak of the Crimean War. That was when cigarette smoking really began. Soldiers returned home from the war, discarded their pipes, and began to roll their tobacco in paper. Possibly this was the worst thing that happened during the whole history of smoking tobacco. No longer was smoking a relaxation or an art. It had become a habit! Tobacco was a way of life, almost as necessary as eating and drinking.

Having briefly traced the course of tobacco since its introduction to our ancestors back in the sixteenth century, let us not depart entirely from *the art of smoking*. Many Aztec paintings depict tobacco being smoked in pipes, and pipes of bone and clay estimated to be over 3,000 years old have been discovered. The North American Indians were possibly the greatest pipe-smokers of all. Mostly their pipes were made of wood, and their very use was a significance of their way of life. Certain pipes depicted peaceable intentions, others warlike. Usually pipes of such importance were kept by the chief for occasions demanding their use. The bowls were large, three or four times the size of those to which we are accustomed, for sometimes as many as fifty natives had to draw from the same fill of tobacco, and if it happened to go out it was considered to be an ill-omen. These ceremonies bear a remarkable likeness to the pipe-smoking competitions mentioned elsewhere in this book.

The North American Indian considered tobacco to be a gift bestowed upon him by the Great White Spirit. Smoking took three forms, religious, social, and purely for one's own pleasure. The leaf was grown along with other crops necessary for survival, and was dried either by the sun or the smoke from cooking fires. The latter was a type of curing, similar to that carried out in Latakia. It was then either cut up with a knife or simply stuffed into the pipe. The resulting smoke could not have been comparable with our modern day processed and blended tobaccos, but nevertheless it *was* pipe smoking. This was where it all originated.

For a long time after Sir Walter Raleigh introduced smoking in England, the usual method of taking tobacco was to light a pipe, draw on it, and puff out the clouds of smoke. No doubt men smoked furiously, and the result was surely a hot and unpleasant flavour, but they persevered simply because it was the fashion. By 1640 the method of 'tobacco drinking' had spread through society. All this was, in actual fact, was *inhaling*. Somebody had discovered that it was far more pleasant and satisfying to swallow the smoke and then to expel it through the nostrils.

Tobacco was finally acclaimed during the Great Plague of London in 1655. Merchants proclaimed it as a medicine. Physicians and all who tended the sick or removed the dead smoked it. Others took to it as a preventative. It was rumoured that only those who smoked tobacco escaped the disease. Smoking was truly established in England.

Tradition has it that philosophers, explorers, and writers all depended upon tobacco for their courage and inspiration. Thomas Carlyle and Frederick Marryat both recommended it but surely Byron's is the best advertisement of all:—

> Sublime tobacco! which, from east to west,
> Cheers the tar's labor or the Turkman's rest,
> Which on the Moslem's ottoman divides
> His hours, and rivals opium and his brides,
> Magnificent in Stamboul, but less grand,
> Though not less loved, in Wapping on the Strand;
> Divine in hookas, glorious in a pipe,
> When tipp'd with amber, mellow, rich, and ripe.

Lord Tennyson, too, was reputedly a heavy smoker, but, like Shakespeare, he made no mention of it in his works. Thackeray claimed that pipe-smoking was a great advantage, particularly during conversation because a man could take his time over replying, without appearing to do so, whilst he drew upon his pipe. He goes as far as to say that not to smoke is a crime!

Many later authors potrayed their own fictional characters as ardent smokers. Sherlock Holmes was seldom without his Persian slipper filled with 'black shag', whilst Allan Quartermain would stuff his pipe with coarse Boer tobacco.

However, in 1773, Johnson claimed that tobacco smoking had gone out of fashion. Possibly he came to this conclusion following the introduction of a new tax on tobacco by Sir Robert Walpole. This tax was only temporary, though, and within a very short time the country was smoking as heavily as ever.

Smoking is something that has been criticised ever since Sir Walter Raleigh's day, and will never be without its opponents. The medical profession now refute the healing qualities of the leaf although many eminent physicians themselves smoke. They associate it with a variety of diseases, yet there are more smokers today than ever before. Non-smoking campaigns are usually restricted to their own band of regular followers, and make little impression upon the hardened lover of the weed. Pipes and cigars are supposedly less harmful than cigarettes simply because they burn at a lower temperature and the smoke is not inhaled. The arguments will rage forever, but tobacco will still be consumed. Legislation would merely drive it underground. The Prohibition era of the United States serves as a lesson in this respect.

PIPES

We have already discussed the very early pipes of the Red Indians, but Europe has a history of its own as far as smoking pipes are concerned. Fifteenth century pipes were very basic. Mostly they were constructed of one half of a walnut shell, in which a hole had been bored, through which a straw was inserted to act as a stem. Clay pipes became increasingly popular after 1600, mostly the kind with long stems, known universally as 'church-wardens'. The wooden pipe was virtually unknown, and it was not until the end of the nineteenth century that the briar pipe was recognised as the finest smoke of all. Its discovery was due purely to chance. A French pipe-manufacturer, holidaying in Corsica, broke his favourite meerschaum pipe, and asked a local craftsman to make him one out of the local wood. This improvisation led to a startling revolution as far as pipe manufacture was concerned. The wood was discovered to smoke cool, with a flavour that enhanced that of the tobacco, and on his return home the Frenchman ordered supplies of briar root to be sent to the village of St. Claude in the Jura mountains. The peasants there were amongst the finest wood-carvers in the world, and within a short time that had turned their skills exclusively to the making of pipes.

The briar used for the making of pipes comes from the root of a tree that is mostly found in the Mediterranean areas. The scorching summer that follows the mild wet winters is responsible for producing the tight grained wood, and the best of these are to be found in those trees growing on steep rocky hillsides. However, good root is not easily nor cheaply obtained. It may take up to 100 years for a root to mature, and some of the best wood for pipe-making has been growing for a quarter of a century. Moreover, many of these trees grow in inaccessible places, and the roots have to be transported for long distances by mule. Only when the wood is cut into blocks ready for pipe-making is it known whether or not it is perfect. Sometimes it is discovered that insects or heath fires have done irreparable damage. Wastage is such that often fifty trees may be needed for the making of *one* briar pipe. Consequently, the price of good briar pipes may range from £5—£100. The quality will be determined by the grain, but if it is just a good smoke that you are seeking then you should find something to suit you in the lower bracket.

People collect pipes in the same way that they collect a variety of other things. Meerschaum, porcelain, ivory, and even animal tusks, may constitute the basic materials for pipe-making. I once came across a meerschaum pipe with an amber stem. Unfortunately, the latter was broken, and on making enquiries about repairs I was staggered to learn that it would cost me in the region of £30.

So, the briar became the favourite amongst pipe-smokers. It is interesting to note that even where comparatively new inventions are concerned, aluminium pipes etc., the bowl is invariably a briar one. It is fortunate, indeed, for us pipe-smokers that that French pipe-manufacturer in Corsica broke his favourite meerschaum!

Smoking has come a long way since 1560. Has it reached perfection, or are there still further delights which will be unravelled to add to the pleasure of the smoker? Only time will tell, but at the moment there is little to surpass the satisfaction to be obtained from a quality briar pipe filled with a carefully selected tobacco.

CHAPTER 9

Snuff

Snuff is the least popular method today of taking tobacco. This does not detract from its pleasures, but, like many other things which were once popular, it has gone out of fashion. The uninitiated are inclined to regard it as a 'dirty habit', but this depends on the snuff-taker. Probably one third of today's smokers have never even sampled snuff.

MAKING YOUR OWN SNUFF

Making snuff from your home-grown tobacco is so simple that it does not warrant a complete chapter of its own. Your leaf must be brittle. This is easily accomplished by drying it in front of a fire until it crumbles at the slightest touch. All that you have to do then is to crush it to a fine powder with a pestle. You will then have the purest form of snuff that it is possible to obtain. Keep it in an airtight tin, using a smaller one to carry your immediate supply in your pocket.

A HISTORY OF SNUFF

It is impossible to say when snuff first originated. Certainly it was being taken in the first half of the seventeenth century, and was often used by those who despised smoking. It was the hallmark of a gentleman, and soon became acceptable amongst women.

There is record of a snuff-grinding mill being in existence near Stoke's Croft, prior to 1750, so it is evident that snuff was being manufactured then on a large scale.

There is an account of two young ladies being robbed by a highwayman on May 5th 1753, during which they suffered a loss of thirty-five shillings and two silver snuff-boxes, so it is evident that during this period the fair sex had discovered the delights of snuff, and, furthermore, it was an accepted practice.

Daniel Defoe wrote that his servant-maid 'took her snuff with the airs of a duchess', and about this time many of the corn mills were being converted to grind snuff. At the Christmas Quarter Sessions in 1756 the Grand Jury at Bourton feared that the change-over to snuff-grinding was detrimental to the welfare of the public. The tenant of the only mill owned by the Corporation was consequently given notice to quit, and it was afterwards advertised as being to let for the sole purpose of grinding corn.

In 1754, William Hulme of Mary-le-port Street took a windmill at Cotham and began making snuff there. Three years later he was declared bankrupt. Surely, this was a sign that snuff was going out of fashion, and smoking was once again being considered a preferable method of taking tobacco. Almost thirty years later, William Cowper wrote:—

Says the pipe to the snuff-box, I can't understand,
What the ladies and gentlemen see in your face,
That you are in fashion all over the land,
And I am so much fallen into disgrace.

Medicated snuff is an excellent antiseptic. Were it taken more widely and frequently it would most certainly help to stop the spread of such germs as that of the common cold. A delicate pinch would go almost unnoticed in a society where many far worse habits predominate.

Notes on Cultivation
(Adapt to Suit Your Requirements)

Year . . . .

Dates: Costs:

Sowing . . . .

Pricking out . . . .

Harvesting . . . .

Curing . . . .

Yield . . . .

Notes:

Notes on Cultivation
(Adapt to Suit Your Requirements)

Year ....

Dates:		Costs:
Sowing		....
Pricking out		....
Harvesting		....
Curing...........................		....

Yield...........................

Notes:

Notes on Cultivation
(Adapt to Suit Your Requirements)

Year ....

Dates: Costs:

Sowing ....
Pricking out ....
Harvesting ....
Curing...........................   ....

Yield...........................

Notes:

Notes on Cultivation
(Adapt to Suit Your Requirements)

Year . . . .

Dates: Costs:

Sowing . . . .

Pricking out . . . .

Harvesting . . . .

Curing. . . . .

Yield. . . . .

Notes: